ADVANCE PRAISE

A LIFE CHANGING read for anyone with something debilitating them from living their life to the fullest... be it a brain injury, a physical injury or illness, depression or a broken spirit. Until I sat down to read *Oh! The Journey*, I don't think I was fully aware I had completely lost myself emotionally and spiritually! Yet, with each page I turned I became more aware that life is truly a journey, not a destination. In its pages I learned to embrace the challenges life throws at us, and understand we are meant to discover the hidden parts of ourselves through them. Bobbie's book motivated me and gave me the courage to get beyond the thought of just existing.

I have known Bobbie all of my life; she was my mother's best friend, but to me... she was one of those rare pictures of a life well-lived! As a leader in both our small community and the beauty industry, Bobbie was a role model for every young girl who wanted to be—and become—something special... she taught me from a very young age to understand beauty from the inside out. I returned to our small town long after her accident, and have witnessed Bobbie's struggles. Thus, reading of them in this book I found her "beauty" once again shining like a beacon for anyone in search of inspiration! It is her story of refusing to accept limits on progress.

She bravely invites readers into her mind, sharing inner thoughts during her long journey to recovery from a traumatic brain injury.

There is a "takeaway" for everyone who reads this book. Hope of recovery, belief in a greater being, inspiration for achieving personal goals, and the courage to face the most difficult of circumstance. For a solid five hours I turned page after page, captivated as I wiped tears from my eyes, and renewed my connection to my life-long mentor. However, the greatest gift was her reminder to me that our "whys" will be answered—we just don't know the when! Thank you Bobbie for helping me reconnect with myself!

~ Samantha Weber
Admin. Exec | Quick-set Auto Glass, Riverton WY

IT WAS AWESOME! *Oh! The Journey* made me cry; it inspired me and I cannot believe what a great person this author is... what she has gone through, what she has accomplished and all she is she is today— is truly amazing.

Even though I personally am no expert on the topic I would think that brain injury people will be helped a lot; her motivation and inspiration will carry them a long way on their personal journey.

~Elaine Bauer
Retired Accountant
State of Montana Dept. of Justice

BOBBIE YEATES' HAS created a true gem in disclosing myriad feelings and emotions associated with being a survivor of traumatic brain injury. She successfully chronicles early emotions she had, plus how she was accepted and (possibly rejected) by those she loved. As the pages unfurl with an unabashed ability to deliver her hurts, gains, successes, and fears through a flowing piece of compelling reading—readers experience what should be truly considered a rare gift.

With great faith, the author conveys that many miracles worked in her life. Many readers will likely be compelled to note Bobbie's honesty as she tells it "like it is" without making the reader feel sorry for her, but to share and cheer for her. Readers will then look around themselves and recognize, perhaps for the first time, friends and family members who may exhibit similar tendencies. Yes, this book can be a tear jerker, and yet, will assist many kindred spirits to better understood as they, too, seek to become more whole and functioning. I wholeheartedly congratulate Bobbie on her efforts!

~T. R. Stearns
Retired Superintendent of Schools

WHAT A TOUCHING, heartfelt book! It will be a blessing to many who have experienced, or currently experience what Bobbie has come forward to share.

I consider Bobbie a dear friend and was touched by her writing and the courage it took to complete this project. You see, I shared a great many experiences with this amazing author both before her accident and in the years since—very aware of the differences in her life following the accident. Her book, however, made me far more aware of the struggles Bobbie faced in dealing with Traumatic Brain Injury; I wish I had known more about it over the years so I might have responded more appropriately, or better understood the "new Bobbie." I know reading her book will help me be more understanding and sensitive to her needs and inner feelings—as other readers will toward their loved ones.

The pages of this book are filled with words of peace and comfort for those with TBI, through a journey and a message that was given Bobbie by God. Her testimony of faith in God, and in the hope of healing, is a gift of powerful inspiration to those suffering from Traumatic Brain Injury. I have always believed, "Every day may not be good, but there is something good in every day." Bobbie proves this proverb with her daily actions and attitudes, and in the beautiful messages found in *Oh! The Journey.*

~ **Virginia King**
Retired, Riverton, WY

*O*H! THE JOURNEY is filled with inspiration and hope for Traumatic Brain Injury (TBI) survivors—and the loved ones who support their healing. Bobbie Yeates takes on the task of helping others understand TBI through her own very real and poignant life experience.

An honest, forthright and uplifting read...

~ **Susan McDonald**
Rocksprings, WY

Oh! The Journey

My Spiritual Path to Thriving with Traumatic Brain Injury

Oh! The Journey

My Spiritual Path to Thriving with Traumatic Brain Injury

BY

Bobbie R. Yeates

Copyright © 2016 by Bobbie Yeates

All rights reserved. No part of this publication may be reproduced, distributed, or transmitted in any form or by any means, including photocopying, recording, or other electronic or mechanical methods, without the prior written permission of the publisher, except in the case of brief quotations embodied in critical reviews and certain other noncommercial uses permitted by copyright law. For permission requests, write to the publisher, addressed "Attention: Permissions Coordinator," at the address below.

Bobbie Yeates
Life is By Design
1009 W Washington
Riverton WY 85201

Ordering Information:
Quantity sales. Special discounts are available on quantity purchases by corporations, associations, and others. For details, contact the publisher at the address above..

Printed in the United States of America

ISBN-13: 978-0692703847 (Life is By Design)
ISBN-10:0692703845

First Edition

14 13 12 11 10 / 10 9 8 7 6 5 4 3 2 1

Cover design by Patrick Sipperly
Book design and production by Voices in Print
Editing by Successfully Published

Disclaimers: Medicine is an ever-changing science. The research and clinical experiences surrounding traumatic brain injury continues to expand our knowledge and awareness, in particular the understanding of its proper treatment. The author, editor and publisher have made every effort to ensure the information in *Oh! The Journey* is in accordance with the "state of knowledge" at the time of its production. They do not assume responsibility for errors, omissions, or consequences from application of the information in the publication, and make no warranty, expressed or implied, with the respect to the contents of the book.

The information in *Oh! The Journey* is true and complete to the best of our knowledge. It is intended as an inspirational and informational guide for those wishing to know more about traumatic brain injuries. It is not intended to replace, countermand or conflict with any advice provided you by your physician. Information in this book stems from personal experience and offers hope and possibilities… not guarantees.

DEDICATION

I DEDICATE THIS book to anyone who believes people with traumatic brain injuries need to have the privilege of information and hope for a healing process that helps them regain lives lost. In recording the path of my recovery, I want them to understand there is normalcy in the many twists and turns of discovery, diagnosis, treatment and therapy when used.

There is hope in the emergence of a new life, even when faced with living forever with the after-effects of traumatic brain injury.

I have written so much in *Oh! The Journey*, but somehow afraid it is not yet enough. I feel there is still so much to share... if I just don't quit. I thought for a very long time I could just hide my feelings, until I found I wear them far too openly to do so. I also discovered there are many "fields" in which to play as we continue on in life, which opens me to dedicating not only my book, but my life passion, to those of you who want to play a bigger game in a life riddled with traumatic brain injury, regardless whether you want to play outfield, base, pitcher, catcher, or shortstop.

Has this been a journey of the mind? Oh, no! This has been a journey of the mind, the heart, the spirit, and my very soul. It will become obvious as you read through the pages of this book that I experienced many things I never anticipated; many days were filled with events and situations I did not ask to have put on my plate. But at the end of the day, I came to embrace the reality that God had saved me, through an accident many now call a miracle, and in that reality I feel blessed for that survival and responsible for sharing that we all live—at some level— a life by design.

LIFE IS BY DESIGN

Well hello, Today!

I open my eyes, look up, smile and say, "Hoo-ray!"

I have this plan, you see... to journey on

Whether it be right or wrong.

Every day we awake is a gift.

Even so very humbled, I say, "I might need a lift."

If we stumble, then take a fall

We have faith, look up and give our Father a call.

Oh! Life's journey has its ups and downs; its ins and outs

But all we have to do is believe this is what Life is all about—

Journey on! Yesterday is gone

The only journey is the one within.

~ Rainer Maria Rilke
German Poet (1875-1926)

TABLE OF CONTENTS

Advance Praise i
Dedication ix
Table of Contents xii
Foreword xv
Preface xix
Acknowledgements xxiii
Introduction xxv
   Where do I fit in here .... *xxv*

A LIFE TRANSFORMED 1
   There are no cooincidences *3*
   A Disconcerted Awakening *6*

NEW BEGINNINGS 13
   Who this book is for? *15*
   How the book is outlined *16*
   WHO is this person that has come to visit me? *22*
   Let the Journey Begin *24*

LIFE'S TRANSITIONS Creating A New You 29
   Diagnosis and Treatment *31*
   TBI in the News *32*
   Medical Research *34*

HELLO! ANYONE HOME? 41
   Who ARE You? *44*
   In the Moment, You Are *45*

I am like a robot	46
Things About Me	47

I AM A SURVIVOR Are You? 51
   Self-Talk and Words 53
   A Deep Dive 59
   Changed Experiences: All is Well 62

I BELIEVE–Do You? 67
   Looking Forward 70
   The Scattered Mind 71
   Truths and Beliefs ⋯ 72

MOMENTS OF TRUTH 75
   Body Image 77
   The Gift of Awareness 77
   Family 78
   Fatigue 80
   Love is… 81
   See Dying As A Gift 81
   Three AM Thoughts 82

A MESSAGE OF FAITH 85
   So many Whys 87
   Fast Forward Three Years 89
   Daily Communication ⋯ 98
   Be inspired by clouds 98
   Beware 99

THE HEALING JOURNAL 101
   A Day Well-Journaled 104
   Dear Diary 106
   Going Social 111
   Finding Clarity in Doodles 115
   About the Author 123

FOREWORD

WHEN IT COMES to TBI's, I have realized there is no "normal," sameness, or parallel universe. Each individual fights his or her own battle for survival.

The journey that Bobbie has been living is extra-ordinary.

Having a head injury as an adult is much different than when you are a child; cell memory will predict outcomes of what the body retrieves. Oftentimes, as an adult, there is a reconnection, but as a child, there is still a building process occurring.

Therapies often will guide what is normal. Work ethic prior to injury is very important; Bobbie had a drive to survive beyond normal. Bobbie's total being transcended, and she is, in many ways... better than before the accident. Time, patience and a lot of hard personal work went into the remodeling of her brain.

In my 43 years of working with TBIs and spinal cord injuries, it is obvious that Bobbie's dedication to recovery is phenomenal—in a word, Bobbie is a shining star! As one of her treating doctors, I am so happy Bobbie has chosen to share her journey with readers; without her faith, this book would never have been possible.

~ Dr. Walter Conard
Doctor of Chiropractic, Naturopathic Doctor, Trained Acupuncturist

under Chiropractic License and a Doctor of Philosophy specializing in Nutrition. Natural Health Solutions, Riverton, WY

In *Oh! The Journey*, Bobbie Yeates has created a book that is a must read for the survivors of the 1.7 million traumatic brain injuries (TBI) sustained annually—and the families and professionals who support them. In July, 2003, she sustained a major, life-threatening TBI in a motorcycle accident... requiring neurosurgery, six days of induced coma, and eighteen days in a referral regional hospital 120 miles away from her home.

Her physical recovery has been described by many as a "miracle." The real inspiration of this insightful book, however, is how Bobbie dealt with the invisible effects of this injury... how it has affected her working memory, her cognition, social interaction, and personal relationships with family.

Through Bobbie's ultimate understanding of the brain's ability to "rewire itself," in a process known as neuroplasticity, her improvement in the invisible effects of this terrible injury—over the past 13+ years—is truly remarkable. She fills in all the blanks that medicines, doctor's visits, and rehabilitation efforts cannot touch.

With her "rewired brain" Bobbie has come to realize she is not alone in this journey, allowing her to be more positive in her life, less anxious through her days, and able to experience improved relationships once damaged. Her memory has improved over the years, in part through the techniques of journaling and doodling, which she describes in some detail in her book.

Bobbie is living proof the brain is not "hardwired," and functioning in predetermined ways, can recover over many years, even when very seriously injured.

This book will inspire readers... giving hope not only to TBI survivors, but to others who have sustained similar "invisible effects" through strokes, neuro-degenerative diseases of the cognitive type (Alzheimer's), and Parkinson's disease... each which effect memory, cognition and social interaction.

I have known Bobbie, her husband Garth, and her family for many years, and feel this book is a seminal addition to our understanding, treatment, and hope for improved quality of life—even with the devastating diagnosis of TBI.

~ Roger L. Gose, MD
Riverton, WY

PREFACE

*O*H! THE JOURNEY is the very book I wish I could have found to help me transition from the life I knew—to the life that was mine to live—following a traumatic brain injury. There are many books that are medically directed, but they leave out the human experiences to which we most naturally relate. I just couldn't find the right combination for the kind of healing, which I felt necessary for my journey... I needed what I looked at as a three-part approach to holistic healing, which would include:

> messages shared by the practitioner,
> voices of the experienced survivor, and
> a spiritual connection to my creator that would hold me, cradled in loving arms.

My purpose in writing *Oh! The Journey* was to become a voice for others who have experienced traumatic brain injury, as shared through my personal experience and growth in the awareness of "all things" TBI. I want to help others increase their own awareness, far more quickly than I was able to; to help them re-set their expectations and live within the realities we face; to answer the unknowns that surface with great frequency, and to deliver a message of hope that readers are not alone... on *their journey*.

Throughout my years of discovery there was an abundance of books as I read, and read... and searched for answers of all the unknowns that accompany traumatic brain injury. I didn't find what I was looking for in the first book I purchased, nor the next. I found myself purchasing first one and then another... always purchasing "the one" I was sure would satisfy my needs.

Often my thoughts would turn to the idea of compiling a little bit of this together with a little bit of that, and then something else I had read somewhere. Then, I thought, maybe I could put "me" back together and finally understand why I can't seem to stay in one complete piece. Unfortunately, the reality remains—I can't! I picture myself as a puzzle with a few pieces missing or misplaced. I was oddly together, yet somehow remained very fragmented and broken.

Oh, the medical books tell me a lot of what happened, what my life is going to be like now, and what it's going to take to "fix" me—why I need this pill or that—my doctors continue to try to fill in the remaining gaps. Over time I have come to understand their words, the ones they share from their studies and the case histories of patients they have assisted following a traumatic brain injury. I have come to respect the compassion many of these physicians show as they help those in need.

And the stories abound in the books I read—of people who experienced some sort of injury themselves and wanted to help others. Somehow these stories inspired me and made me feel much less like a loose cog in life, but still... something was missing. I wasn't getting what I needed; they lacked something I couldn't quite distinguish.

Finally, after really giving my quandary considerable thought, I had an ah-ha moment—I needed to write a book that would fill in the many discomforting gaps. It would be a combination of the medical intellect and the unique experiences of a life lived with traumatic brain injury, and it would provide hope, inspiration and guidance—all the things that have been part of my journey to reclaim my life, no matter how altered it may have been. It would be my hope and prayer that the pages of my book would help you reflect on your own experience, to once again look at yourself with a smile, even when a tear or two trickles down your face as you struggle to remember something, but quickly write it down because you are oh, so afraid you might forget.

My belief in our heavenly father has been the foundation of my walking this journey. He has helped me along this extended path, on which there have been many twists and turns, countless ups and downs; He has fostered the belief such that my faith has never faltered.

I want you to be comfortable with the questions life throws at you and to use them to your advantage. I most certainly have questions each and every day and know they will be answered; I just have to be ok with not knowing the when.

> *I do believe we are meant to discover the hidden parts of ourselves, correct what we don't like, and improve upon what we do.*

It is my prayer *Oh! The Journey* is down to earth and will help you look forward to tomorrow—as you choose to enjoy today—and go about your future with a promise of discovering you.

ACKNOWLEDGEMENTS

MY LOVE AND deepest thanks go out to all those people who love and believed in me throughout this venture...

Garth...

> my husband, the father of our beloved children, our grandchildren's Papa, and most importantly—my best friend, my confident and partner in life and all eternity. I thank you for being there with all my love, heart and soul, and for always saying, even though we can remain individuals, "We are one." We have always worked together—as one—that is our unity; I have always been independent and that retains our individuality.

My children...

> Rocky
> Heather
> Tiffany
> Garth Jr.
> Maygen
> Talon

And... all the grandchildren whom you've given me as the greatest gift of all. What a blessing! You are all a significant part of this book... whether you realize it or not.

My sibling...

> Tim Burke, and the rest of my immediate family, each of who has passed on and awaits me in Heaven and my extended family—aunts, uncles, nieces and nephews.

My friends...

> with whom I have been blessed—far too many to list! Although I do not call out your names here, you can know in your heart you are included and I cherish the journey we have had, and will continue in the future.

There were days I felt alone in my journey, experiencing shame, pain, confusion and the unfortunate awareness I was not, nor possibly would I ever be, the person who came to this TBI party, but throughout this time, I have grown to love the new person I became as a result of the accident.

Let's move forward on a journey we can share, taking a path through some of the transformational things I want you to discover and love about the "now" you!

Introduction

Where do I fit in here

WE HAVE TO believe deeply we can overcome whatever adversities are thrown our way. We have to believe our heavenly father will guide us. He has never said it would be easy; just that it would be worth it. To understand, we must first open our hearts and our minds — and just believe — and then take life step-by-step.

I have a head injury. Unfortunately, that injury came to me in a "suitcase" full of other things I have to deal with: anger, distress, the constant need to wonder why, and each day I seem to pull from it new discoveries that are not always comfortable for me. It is as though someone other than myself packed that suitcase, and when I pull something from it... I have to be prepared for a possible setback. I stand back and look a-glance at the troublesome items and find that nothing can stand in the way of my belief; all the burdens and struggles stuffed inside are nothing more than my being tested in life.

It is not easy to have this conversation, with myself or with you, but — because I continue to believe — I invite you to share my journey and discover for yourself how *you can thrive* even when a Traumatic Brain Injury has been part of the lot you have drawn in life. Just as I learned, you will find for yourself it will not be easy... but it will be worth it.

At this moment in life, you have to choose how you will continue to respond or react to the changes in your life—even when they fill you with fear, confusion, anger or a surplus of feelings—which previously were not your constant companions.

Life is an ever-changing process; nothing is final. Even when I think seriously about my injury and the resultant trauma, I find hope in knowing each and every day can be mine... to start life anew each and every day.

As my trauma found a resting place, I found I wanted to be alone at times. I found solace appreciating it is ok to hide away and shield myself from too many questions; questions for which I had absolutely no responses.

Faith remains my greatest gift; it is gracious and from God. This gift was the grace of trusting and knowing I could cling to the promise that one day... all things would work to my favor.

I am a Survivor! I have a dear friend who reminds me to ask myself, "Did I live, did I love, and did I matter?" Through all the fog-like mist in a symbolic dark forest, I discovered the answer to that question was, "I am to share the struggles of my experience with others so they can find benefits in the same discoveries that turned darkness, pain, anger and countless other discomforting thoughts to hope—based on setting new goals for my life, conquering multiple challenges, and remaining diligent to a journey where, by my design, I would have a life that served me... and others! There was a beautiful, pivotal, life-changing moment when I realized I was strong and confident in the knowing that in sharing my story, there would be others whose hearts would be set on a journey of healing because they discovered someone else has been there—done that.

Gospel Singer, Gloria Gaither, once wrote of her reasons for a journey. She noted that we may run, walk, stumble drive or fly; however, in her wisdom she also advised we should never lose sight of the reason for the journey, or to miss an opportunity to see a rainbow on the way. I am glad to have seen my share of rainbows on my journey, and pray you will come to embrace the inspiration hidden within Gaither's words and in the pages of *Oh, The Journey*.

Oh! The Journey

My Spiritual Path to Thriving with Traumatic Brain Injury

A LIFE TRANSFORMED

*My goal is always transformation.
I love to watch people transform their lives,
which includes their inner world and their
outer world.*

Debbie Ford (1955-2013)
American Author

Oh! The Journey | Bobbie R. Yeates

MY STORY BEGINS with the simple things I can remember... things like a beautiful weekend which was a regular occurrence for our family... gathering together to leave our work-week behind. We had traveled from Riverton to Dubois (Wyoming) to spend our days playing out doors and enjoying the beauty of nature. It moves beyond those cherished moments to the tragedy of a motorcycle accident that left both my husband and me seriously injured and our lives forever transformed as I was diagnosed with Traumatic Brain Injury (TBI).

To introduce you then, to the transformation of my life... marred, as you will, by an accident resulting in TBI, I can best do so by sharing a letter received following that event, written by a woman to whom I am forever grateful for most likely saving my life. I believe her words unfold my story as I could never do.

THERE ARE NO COOINCIDENCES...

April 16th, 2005

Hi Bobbie,

I am sorry this has taken so long... but life just happens. You asked me to write to you and tell you what I remember about your accident.

We were on the way to Riverton, Wyoming, to take my husband's (Joe) mother to see her sister, Ann Burns. We were going to travel through Jackson Hole, but as we were nearly there, we were stopped and turned around because of a forest fire. As we passed through Dubois, it was late afternoon—early evening. I was sitting in the back seat when my husband said, "Oh, No! There has been a motorcycle accident."

We stopped and jumped out; I could see the motorcycle lying on its side as the dust began clearing—the wheels still spinning. Looking around, I did a quick assessment. I had been an EMT 2-D, and worked on an ambulance for ten years. Your husband was sitting up, holding his right arm. I told Joe to stay with him; you were lying face down in the dirt. I could see enough of your face to see you were breathing, and that you most likely had a severe head injury. As you were unconscious and bleeding a large amount from your mouth and nose, I called Joe over, and showed him how to hold your neck and head in traction while I checked you for other life threatening injuries—of which I found none.

I ran back over and quickly assessed your husband, who was in shock and kept asking, "What happened?" and "Is Bobbie alright?"

I thought your husband probably had an arm or shoulder injury and possible head injury as both your helmets were lying scattered on the ground, it was pretty obvious they had not been worn during the accident.

I then ran back to you and took over traction of your neck and head and sent Joe back to your husband. By now, there were several bystanders stopped, and someone had called 911. I was very worried about you, and kept talking to you, and praying over you. Several people wanted to turn you over, but I would not let them because there was too much bleeding from your mouth, and there was no one there who know the proper procedure on how to "log roll" you. I laid protectively over you—talking and praying until you regained consciousness for a short time, and when you shared your name was "Bobbie."

Oh! The Journey | Bobbie R. Yeates

We stayed with the both of you until the ambulance arrived and they took over your care when we finally got back inside our vehicle. We prayed again for you before we left. That night when we arrived at Joe's aunt and uncle's (George and Ann Burns), Joe's Aunt Ann said she didn't know where Ken was. "He said he would be here and Ken always keeps his word!"

The next night Ken came over and apologized for not coming the night before since a special prayer meeting had been called because some friends had been in a serious motorcycle accident the evening before just outside Dubois. He further mentioned you had been flown to a larger hospital because of severe head injuries. Joe and I looked at each other in a state of shock... we knew it was God's hand.

If we had not been turned around before Jackson Hole;

If I had not had experience as an EMT, we might have caused further injury and/or death;

If Ken Burns had not have been in the prayer group we would never have known what happened to you.

As Christians, we know there are no coincidences with God! I know He directed us to be there with you. We are so blessed to know you have recovered, and remain in awe of God, our Father.

We are so happy things worked out for you; if there is anything we can do or help you with, let us know. I am happy to learn you are helping others.

We pray God richly blesses you both. Please call or write and let us know how things are going.

God Bless You,

Dee

P.S. When you regained consciousness and said your name was Bobbie, you also asked what happened. I told you, "You hit a guardrail and were thrown off your motorcycle, but you are going to be fine."

You then said, "Oh, I know we're going to be fine, I just wondered what happened!" Then you lost consciousness again.

I still often wonder, "How *did* I know we were going to be fine?"

A Disconcerted Awakening

OBVIOUSLY I WAS not—could not—be aware of the events immediately following the accident. I can only rely on others around me to fill in the gaps. One of those was a creative writing paper my son Garth, Jr. wrote, and which I so proudly share with you here.

I **HAVEN'T SLEPT** *for over 36 hours now and Juan Valdez is knocking on the door to open my eyes and wake me up. Unfortunately, this is not a dream. As I look over my beautiful mother's motionless body here in the Casper hospital, I'm waking up. As I look at her gorgeous face cluttered with breathing apparatuses and mildly disfigured by immense swelling, already plainly visible, I do start to awaken. I think about my beaten and battered father who is laid up in the Riverton hospital 120 miles from the greatest love of his life. Despite several broken bones, he suffers more mentally— worrying about his life mate, my mother.*

I now find myself suffering from so much worry and empathy that my stomach is in knots as it gets harder and

Oh! The Journey | Bobbie R. Yeates

harder to breathe. It's been so long since I felt any empathy; I begin to wonder how I became so cynical. I remember the heartbreaking event that reduced me to the cynic that now looks back at me in the mirror. I've tried so hard to block it out of my mind, but now it only hurts me more to think I let something childish change my life. Now I feel even more disheartened when I think that what happened with the only people who have always been there for me is the only way I could wake up. Why couldn't I stay in my disillusioned world of contempt where I looked out for number one and number one alone?

I don't want to hear that people think movies, the media, or even rap music are the cause of my blatant disregard for each other's feelings or well being. Although I know that isn't the problem, I am also not naïve enough to disregard the fact everyone's lives are moderately sculpted by the media icons and essential figures that we see everyday. I also know these icons only bring us to the water.

The accident was like something out of a movie, which explains my disbelief. The movie was set like this: The two beautiful people representing my parents are headed home to their family after a short weekend vacation to the mountains. It's a cool summer day in the heart of Wyoming as Garth, Sr. and Bobbie Yeates travel home after a weekend-long four-wheeling excursion. They travel speedily on the windy but well-banked highway from x-random point A to x-random point B on their 1998 Honda Goldwing. The 1500 cc motorcycle handles the drastic curves as though it was what the bike was made for. As the couple comes to a 90-degree turn banked up against the Red Rock cliffs, the bike gradually slows.

Then, in an uncontrollable instant, the cruise control reengages, standing the bike completely upright... enabling the powerful man to lean into the corner. The powerful machine

Oh! The Journey | Bobbie R. Yeates

slams into the guardrail, riding the pipes like a locomotive set on tracks... pulling the bike through the corner. When the once beautiful Goldwing reaches the end of the guardrail, its rear wheel spins out on the loose gravel... thrusting the bike sideways and laying it down at 70 miles per hour.

My father takes the entire initial blow, tearing his arm out of socket, leaving it dangling and burying him into the ground on his back so all he can do is sit and watch the bike spin to the back wheel and endo—with my mother still aboard. She bounced and rolled with the speed and weight of the bike crushing her frail body. With my father lying in a pool of his own blood, slightly concussed and unable to walk, there is nothing to imagine but the worst. A concerned cowboy drops his old Chevy pickup into a lower gear while slamming on the breaks to rush to the presumably dead couple.

The storyboard then advances instantaneously to my father's eyes, which look upon the flashing lights of an ambulance, and the muffled voice of a medical attendant demanding he lie still. They tell him about my incoherent mother, and how she has already been boarded on the first arriving ambulance, and will be in a life flight helicopter to a first rate hospital soon. Nothing hurts him more than his broken heart on the ambulance ride, where he feels completely responsible for the death of his lover.

Oh, my god! This isn't a movie; this is what happened. How can this be? Bloody car accidents only happen in multi-million dollar action flicks. My parents cannot die like this; my siblings and I cannot be left alone so young. There is no earthly explanation and no exact description, so how can it be real? Is it god's fault? How could he let this happen if he truly exists?

Maybe I should pray, but I haven't led a good enough life; god would never answer a prayer from me... that is unless I

Oh! The Journey | Bobbie R. Yeates

plead with him to do it for them, and not for me. I feel my eyes getting wider as my mind drifts. I start to think of all the good times I had, and wonder if I would have sinned so frequently if I knew I would be forced to ask god for a favor as great as this one. I think about all this and the hardest part still remains the necessity of my dis-concern and apparent strength. I must flex my muscle, hide my emotion, and try to bury my younger sister's tears in my bicep. Someone must be strong... I wish it wasn't me.

It is now hour 40 and I am back in Riverton at my father's side—hardened with the task of being the bearer of bad news. As my lips tremble, and I struggle to keep eye contact, I mutter the words, "Things got worse Dad, and Mom is just about to go in for brain surgery." I tried to explain that things would be ok and they were going to save her life, but I couldn't find the right words as I gazed upon my father's tears. He is the ultimate "tough guy." In 21 years I had never seen him do anything more than wince. Never a tear, a "Damn, that hurts," but here he is... laying in his hospital bed with a dislocated shoulder, three broken vertebrae, four broken ribs, one broken ankle, a deep laceration on his chin, and a side covered in road rash—pretending his concussion isn't fazing him and the most painful thing is the tears rolling down his puffy cheeks.

Right now, I can't talk to my father; it hurts too badly. Fortunately for me, there is always someone watching and always someone who actually gives a damn. Around here—the community where I have lived and grown—you can always find someone to help, regardless how serious or minimal the problem is. Even if all you need to do is find someone to talk to, it is possible to find someone who will actually listen to you, as opposed to just sitting and waiting for their turn to talk. It represents an idea, which every man of every faith can embrace.

Oh! The Journey | Bobbie R. Yeates

I bring up faith because of a horrific realization that slapped me in the face. How scary would it be for you if when you finally needed a prayer answered, you had to wonder if you have been a good enough person thus far in your life to make such a request. Trying to plead to God right after you cursed his name for trying to take one of his angels back when you weren't ready to lose her. Mentally forcing you to refurbish your prayer and ask for whomever your prayers are directed at to do it for "them" and not for "you" because you are afraid the powers that be won't listen if it's you asking!

You never know when it will happen to you. You never know when you may receive on of those heart-attack-causing phone calls; I pray you never do, but then again... who am I to ask for even that/ As I try to bring my new-found enlightenment to the surface, I preach my revelations just as Bhodi-Dharma did when he finally went to the east. I must also say that as I non-believer, I do now feel blessed. I use the term non-believer with the thought that I was never lucky enough to be born with faith. I am an abstract person but I, on the same note, do need concrete facts if I am going to base my life on a particular belief. I'm not going to start going door-to-door preaching to anyone, spoon-feeding our community with my enlightened propaganda, because it is this community that makes me feel so blessed. I would have nothing and be nothing if it were not for my friends, my family, and the warmth in the hearts of those who surround me.

I also feel blessed the staff at Riverton Memorial Hospital worked so swiftly and with such perfection. They alone can be honored with the credit for my mother's recovery; when it happens, that is. The neurosurgeon in Casper said himself that Mom was handled perfectly.

I wonder if this would have been possible without all the people that helped me pray. Just when I think the world cannot get more cynical, something like this happens and our community's strength comes... knit together like the tightly knotted links on a piece of medieval chain mail. I only hope it isn't short-lived. I don't want to say things such as: "Well, I guess I'll hear from you again the next time someone I love is on their death bed." I am now closer to so many people, and I want it to stay that way. We all live here together; we may as well love living here together.

I think about my son's transformation during the early days of my medical trauma and how much love and caring he exhibited. I liken the caring of Garth, Jr. to the words of the amazing author and motivational speaker, "Leo" Buscaglia, PhD, "Too often we underestimate the power of a touch, a smile, a kind word, a listening ear, or the smallest acts of caring, all of which have potential to turn a life around."

Today, I want to send a message to a world afraid to interact with a loved one who may experience this silent, invisible disorder... reach out to them with acts of caring.

NEW BEGINNINGS

When we dream alone it is only a dream, but when many dream together it is the beginning of a new reality.

~ Friedensreich Hundertwasser (1928-2000)
Austrian Architect.

WHO THIS BOOK IS FOR?

BRAIN INJURED PEOPLE, family members, spouses, friends, neighbors and professional peers, physicians and other healthcare providers, attorneys who may have the privilege to represent people suffering from TBI, health insurance companies who have to deal with medical coverage, employers who have to implement employee-related options in the workforce, and other support system members and organizations.

This book is for you if...

You need yet to discover there is a natural timetable in the healing process for brain trauma. Your task is to plant your seeds for the tomorrow you want. Have patience, for the seeds will not pop up or sprout on the next day. The process will be slow, and you must willingly nourish what surfaces, give it sunlight, check it daily and know it is growing and before you are aware... you will find beautiful blossoms of a new and better life. It just takes time.

You are concerned with how your brain injury affected your relationship with your loved ones. Trust me, virtually everyone has reacted differently to me—and in retrospect—me to them. Stress, anger and frustration, family dynamics, 1:1 communications, and how I ultimately chose to connect with them.

You experience feeling angry, uncomfortable, abandoned, helpless, unloved, ignored, depressed, vulnerable, and less important to those whom you feel should love you most, as you give in to frustration or being emotionally numb.

HOW THE BOOK IS OUTLINED

SHORTER CHAPTERS, DEALING with specific topics is how this book is laid out—some of which will apply to your experience and others, which hopefully you may never have to suffer through. During your reading, you will come to recognize various levels of recovery... some of which you will ultimately resolve; some that may feel like additional complexities in your life.

Anxiety... I discovered some side notes I had written specifically about anxiety that should be shared here so you might relate to your own anxious moments.

Will it ever go away? One moment I am fine, yet in the simple flip of a coin I'm off and running another attack—why? What triggers them? I frighten so easily because the brain trauma is so hard to accept, not only for myself, but for all those around me. Every time I have an attack, it not only hurts me, but my family as well. I know they are praying for it to just go away; I do that myself! I also know they are asking the same question, "Why?" What is the trigger point? Is it alcohol, sugar, noise, commotion, atmosphere, fear?

We all need to make a list; a checklist, I tell myself. So, every time you have an attack, make a note of where you have been, what you have consumed... anything you think may have triggered an attack. By taking the time to remember and relate events to issues, we are better able to work through the attacks, learning how to handle the dilemma and patting ourselves on the back for facing the fear and anxiety. Quite frankly, I know there is a possibility they will never go away or totally disappear, but anything that works as a coping mechanism is a giant step forward!

There are many forms of anxiety; I personally have experienced several. Never a dull moment around me! As I write "Oh! The Journey," I am fully embracing the reflection on the past decade plus since my accident. Some of the memories may be from a year ago; others yesterday or even a few hours ago. Although sometimes it is healthy to take a trip down memory lane and find incidents to identify with, and perhaps decide how something might be "fixed," basically I have adopted the belief that if it is in the past; it has already happened, nothing can change that, so just leave it there.

Learning self-love (self-care) is, I believe, an integral part of healing; it is the point of connection when you love yourself deeply — and believe you can once again "thrive" in life — that healing begins. One of my journaled pages focused specifically on this message, and I believe it was truly a pivotal moment when things started on a much more comforting path on my long, long journey.

Love thyself. Nourish the seeds of growth within you. Today, I claim this as my mantra.

Wow! What is going on? I have to admit I am more than just a little frightened. I personally have tried to accept everything that has happened to me in the past and I feel I have successfully done that, but Garth challenges me to consider why I am angry with him. Today, I know why! It isn't any one thing, but an accumulation of things occurring over three decades:

The 4-wheeler wreck we had with Tiffany and Stormy — Garth told me to keep up and I tried, but Tiffany grabbed the brake when we were going up the hill. We stopped and went backwards and the 4-wheeler came down on top of me. I was hurt and bleeding, yet Garth was upset with me. Am I to be passive and just feel that "life goes on?"

Garth, Garth Jr. and I were snowmobiling and found ourselves in a whiteout. Heading back we lost Garth Jr. and this 'momma" came undone! I was surprised, as a parent, that Garth was upset with me. We had to go for help and all he could say to me was "You have to keep up!" It seemed I just couldn't, and while trying I hit a big patch of ice, lost my grip on my machine and went over the top, which knocked me out. Garth came back, and got me back on my machine, telling me, "You have to drive it back." I did; I was hurt again—concussion. Going to a different doctor and feeling beyond helpless, we found Dr. Wirt in Ft. Collins... he fixed me and I felt, "Life goes on."

And then... the motorcycle accident on July 13th, 2003. We took the motorcycle to Dubois, trying to prove to Garth I wasn't scared to ride with him on it. After a big day of 4-wheeling with our grandkids, it was late... I was tired and didn't want to ride the motorcycle home. Garth retorted to my refusal, saying, "No. You wanted to ride it up, you will ride it home." The wreck—we didn't make it home and I will never be the same again, but "Life goes on."

All of these things added up and I knew this was the core of an anger that did not support self-love or healthy self-care. So many things—all mixed up with feelings from over three decades. All in all I love Garth deeply; when I said yes for all eternity I meant it. What happened in some ways made me feel unworthy, but I cling to knowing I have done everything in my power to be the best I can be... to be the best daughter, wife, mom, and nana. I know I have ups and downs as does everyone in life and I question, "Is our heavenly father just challenging me every day?" I accept the challenges willingly for my love

Oh! The Journey | Bobbie R. Yeates

for our Lord is so strong, as is my love for his son, Jesus Christ.

I do know you cannot fully love yourself if you harbor anger toward another and am grateful Garth understood this and ultimately helped me break the ties anger held on me. I believe I had the last few episodes for a particular reason; I just wasn't sure why. I hold no more anger with what happened in the past; I believe that anger was Satan lurking around trying to come into my life. No chance! In fact, Garth gave me a blessing that was so strong—literally telling Satan to be gone and never to return. I believe completely in the Lord's power—transmitted through Garth—I just didn't know there was so much anger pent up in me, but I now believe it is gone.

Come Fly with Me

I used to dream of my perfect mate
One that would love me forever
Always knowing it was never too late
Spreading our wings, learning to fly
Sometimes too low, and others way to high
But always flying as one
Holding tight and thinking,
this is so much fun
No matter what the season brings
We'll survive because we have wings
Whether it be stormy or shun shiny weather
We are one and we'll always be together
My love… come fly with me
And forever fill my heart with glee
There's o end to the sky,
Hang on, its time to fly

Brain injury recovery therapy—I chose not to engage in therapy. In looking back, what drove me to that choice was feeling I was being unloved, as though I had done something wrong and I just wanted to be home where I could feel the emotional support I had previously found common there. Not too terribly long ago, I had reason to reach out to my original physician, and... well, let me just say he was not happy that I had not returned for all the assistance he would have been able to provide me. Would my story have been different? Perhaps.

Fighting back! You can trust me that there will be a time when you will decide to fight back! Fight against whatever caused the traumatic brain injury; fight against what your brain causes you to do; fight back for the answers to help you break through the trauma and arrive at all you can be, and perhaps, in some miraculous way, *all you were meant to be.*

You can also trust me that:

When you fight back, you will discover that pieces of you will be different, but those different pieces will be other parts you can learn to love, support and use to enhance your life. You will see new pieces of you as they emerge, but if you are not aware this is all a part of the process, you may experience discovering these new nooks and crannies frustrating—even though fascinating at times.

The idea is to embrace the "now" you, not mourn what you feel you have lost.

If you make it your ultimate quest to "love" the "now" you—as you show up each day—you will find this the key that unlocks the door to emerge from your pain, and pass into the pleasure of your new "being."

Challenges exist for everyone in life. You may feel you have been elected the trauma candidate of the day for too many days in succession, but you are *not alone.*

Although you are swept up in discomforting feelings: embarrassment, lacks of dignity, and being devalued by the invisible struggle inside, you have to want your life back!

WHO IS THIS PERSON THAT HAS COME TO VISIT ME?

CONSIDER THE fact that although I was perfectly fine on the outside, yet forever changed in the brain that made me who I was, the biggest burden to bear, and with it—with this new person that seemingly came to "visit" me—came the following disruptive, disheartening and immobilizing things:

I could no longer:

Follow conversations or track sequential concepts

Follow directions—got lost on the way to places I used to drive to subconsciously

Recognize people

Solve simple problems

Control my comments; often blurting out inappropriately

In fact, if you had asked me when I first started taking on the challenge to "manage" my verified traumatic brain injury, my life represented:

Mass confusion—*at most everything I used to find comfortable…*

Oh! The Journey | Bobbie R. Yeates

***Short attention span**—needed sticky notes and lists just to exist...*

*An inability to **recall basic details**...*

*The kind of **prevailing doubt** that began to cloud my intellect...*

*A life filled with pervasive feelings of **being trapped in a body I didn't belong in** and living in a world where I felt I had been abandoned...*

*My **no longer being sure of exactly who** I was, where I could go, who I might turn into, or what... if I should happen to get this right, what that would even look like...*

I do want to share the hope with you, however... a kind of hope that was never-ending and ultimately embraced as my life evolved through:

*The very soul of me that **was tenacious and believed** I was strong enough to manage even this part of my life journey...*

***Studying various "healing systems"** that might provide new answers for me; new directions to help put me back on track...*

*A **passion** that begged me to not become a cliché—or a person people stared at, condemned or felt sorry for...*

*Learning to **notice the loss, but live with** it. I had to embrace that I 'used' to be smarter, more capable, more social... more this, more that.*

At the end of the day, my greatest shift toward thriving was the moment I stopped and thought, Bobbie, who are you now, where do you want to go from here?

LET THE JOURNEY BEGIN

NOT ONLY do I want to make sense of what I experienced, but to offer hope to readers that someone who has experienced a Traumatic Brain Injury can not only survive the occurrence, but learn to thrive, and as I have been able to do, live my life by design.

This book is made possible because I continue to... live life to the fullest I can each day! When my editor asked me a lengthy series of questions about how my journey began and a short summary of what has transpired, I really had to stop and do the deep dive! But, I think the following will cover the kinds of things you have either experienced, or will have the privilege to at some point in your own journey.

*Just remember,
every journey begins with the first step...*

Can I say I have now returned to a level of activity fairly close to my pre-accident level? *I am so grateful and feel fortunate my activity level is very close to the same as it was before our accident. I want to go... to be... to be involved... have fun and be a part of everything. I have to be honest here—I truly needed some "time out" but quickly realized I was ready and willing to get up and get going again. What a great feeling that was! Finding myself arising on a new day and feeling it was a blessing. What is so great is if I don't remember something, or understand it... I am no longer afraid to ask.*

My journey has included a lot of highs and lows—just in understanding the different forms of love that was shown to me along the way. Each occasion was a totally different event, therefore how friends and loved ones treated me was unalike, which didn't help me fully understand and often left me off on a pursuit to answer new questions.

*We must remember whatever we happen to do in life is not always a one-way street, and we are **not alone**! I have lapsed many times in my journey, and may continue to do so, but so do people who are not challenged by Traumatic Brain Injury. I liken this understanding to the reality that even though we may be injured and sometimes feel life is, or perhaps should be, all **about us**—that is just not the case! We are **not alone**, but not in the sense of others always being there to support us. They suffer right alongside us and there should be days we recognize the needs of others and give all we can—on the days we can—so they, too, have the comfort of **knowing they** are not alone. There are, indeed, always going to be others who walk your journey with you... beside you... and it may take time to move beyond your healing and slowly see how they live, love, and matter in your life. My ultimate hope is you feel the different kinds of love exhibited around you as others support the path you must now walk.*

When did I first realize there was something wrong with my brain? *When I was still in the hospital strange things were being required of me, knowing I was injured from the accident. Why did I have to bathe myself? Why was I instructed to make muffins and being asked what my favorite foods were—taking me out to lunch and then bringing me back to the hospital? Oh! and I had to bounce balls and they wanted me to go on to Denver... like something was wrong. Why did my family not want me? It was time for them to decide what to do with me.*

I honestly cannot remember being told I had Traumatic Brain Injury; I only remember wanting Tiffany to bring me home... knowing somehow I would be safe there. If I had a crystal ball and knew what I really needed at that time, I would have followed the instructions to go to Denver where there would be more medical support for me.

I really do not recall much of my first year at all. I do know I was besieged with headaches, dizziness and a much diminished capacity to walk. Even getting out of bed and walking down the stairs was a task. I know I wanted everything to be ok, and went back to work—where everything was totally different. I knew who I was before was a person in control and ok with things; the person I was in that time frame, however, couldn't handle all the commotion and noise and not being able to "fix" myself!" Little did I know that my brain was in charge! The only way to be at my peak potential again was to listen to my brain.

What do you think it would feel like... to wake up each and every morning, filled with a constant fear and wondering, "Who will I upset today?" It was frightening, disheartening, and a real blow to my normal level of self-confidence to not know why I upset others, or how to keep my relationships in a healthy balance. Thankfully, with each day... with each courageous step forward... each of these issues became less of a burden and I was able to regain the things I was so fearful of having lost.

If you were not in denial about your experiences and injuries, what was your motivation to take whatever action necessary to be better? *My motivation was going to the seminars being held in the State of Wyoming and the National Conference... representing our state. The things I learned at these events made me very aware of what my condition was, what my options were, and what I could look forward to if I chose to walk the journey rather than succumb to the alterative —***doing nothing short of existing***. I would encourage every person to look for the inner desire to help others – know you*

Oh! The Journey | Bobbie R. Yeates

can see others who are wondering themselves how to make this altered life happen. It is when you get outside yourself, and serve as a role model for others who want to ask for help, but don't know how to... and it is when you let your life be a message, or a beacon to someone else, that you truly start on a journey you can be confident will be a forward-direction and never-ending.

Trust me, you will heal more each time you hear someone say, "You are such a miracle; you so inspire me!"

LIFE'S TRANSITIONS
CREATING A NEW YOU

Sometimes the transition from being in control of your life to having absolutely no control is swift, but other times it is so gradual that you wonder exactly when it truly began.

~**Mickey Rooney** (1920-2014)
American author and actor.

FOR YOU, ME, or others to fully understand the dynamics of traumatic brain injury, and be able to fully tap into the healing power, it is necessary to look at certain medical aspects. Some of what follows is what I read about in the many books I read, some things I learned from my doctors, and a

DIAGNOSIS AND TREATMENT

MY ORIGINAL DIAGNOSIS and treatment are still rather a blur to me for the most part. There are days when having a conversation with someone, a memory will spark for a scant moment and I scramble to journal that momentary recall. I know, from conversations with my family I was in an induced coma for six days following my surgery, but my daughters were in my room when I awakened. At this time, I know I experienced one of the greatest reality checks of my entire life... "What is going on?" Once the nurse realized I was awake, I she asked me, Bobbie, Do you know the girls at the foot of your bed?"

I looked down and promptly responded, "Of course I do! They are my daughters, Heather, Tiffany and Maygen." I may not have been aware of other medical issues or concerns that would present themselves in the coming days, and I may not have understood what was going on, but I sure knew my girls! They started crying, somehow knowing I had made a turn for the better and I guess I knew, just as at the site of the accident, that "everything was going to be ok." I was sure my daughters would enlighten me... and all would be well.

Oh! The Journey | Bobbie R. Yeates

TBI IN THE NEWS

As I personally experienced, Traumatic brain injuries (TBIs) can be the most devastating injury a person can suffer in an accident. Many, like myself, suffer lasting physical and cognitive damage. Head injuries similar to mine can make it difficult to recall old memories or remember new information, making it next to impossible to communicate as comfortably as what was once possible, and in so many ways, forever change personalities. One key lesson I did learn from my experience is that no one in life is safe from TBIs; no one is immune. Fame, nor fortune, offers protection from a brain injury. They affect people of every age, gender, socioeconomic sector, religion or political party. Although some activities, such as sports, increase your risk, falls, accidents, vehicle collisions and being assaulted cause most TBIs. From actresses to politicians, from athletes to musicians—each suffered as acutely at I have... struggled with the same challenges of brain injuries that every sufferer faces.

We each suffer injuries in circumstances beyond our control. Tragically, many die from the injuries—others simply live a life forever altered. I found hope in researching "people in the news" knowing the public may become more aware of the struggles that all TBI patients face, and pray their hearts are opened to others whose lives will never be the same.

You can read about Bob Woodruff, who joined ABC News in 1996 and covered major stories throughout the country and around the world. Highly successful in his career, Woodruff was named co-anchor of ABC's "World News Tonight" in December 2005. Unfortunately, on January 29, 2006, while reporting on U.S. and Iraqi security forces, Woodruff was seriously injured by a roadside bomb that struck his vehicle near Taji, Iraq... and, in the world of TBI—the rest is a history to which many of can relate. *In an Instant: A Family's Journey of Love and Healing* Paperback —published February 12, 2008 by Lee and Bob Woodruff can be found on Amazon. He was as a seminar I was at in Bethesda, Maryland, and was teaching there.

The life changes faced by Gold medal winning Olympian, James Cracknell, who suffered a serious brain injury in 2010 while filming in Arizona for a TV show, were not all that much different than my own

In his book, *Touching Distance*, James and his wife Beverley share the circumstances following his brain injury. James developed epilepsy, memory problems and completely lost his sense of taste. I could relate to his feeling a significant change in personality, losing his temper quickly and becoming heated and aggressive. The story is a candid revelation of the effect of James's brain injury on their marriage and family life.

I could also relate to James' drive and a competitive nature that kept him reaching for further achievements in spite of his brain injury. I was also challenged by Cracknell's interest in supporting Headway, the Brain Injury Association responsible for raising awareness about brain injury and its effects.

Oh! The Journey | Bobbie R. Yeates

Former BYU football player and NFL quarterback for the San Francisco 49ers, Steve Young is taking a stand for a united front about TBI in professional sports. The NFL Hall of Famer experienced seven concussions before retiring in 1999; he is reported to have suffered many TBI symptoms. Young, now a football analyst for ESPN, recently contributed to the documentary "League of Denial: The NFL's Concussion Crisis," speaking not only about his experiences, but also his concern for current and future players.

Medical Research

IT IS IMPOSSIBLE for me to write *Oh! The Journey* without adding medical information. I know there have been days when I totally understood what my physician shared with me; there have been others when I shopped around bookstores and online for more information to satisfy my growing questions. In the beginning you don't know what you don't know, and the more aware you become, the more you try to fill in the gaps between doctor-speak and a layman's understanding. This section, then is intended to share with you a small portion of the many pages I've read, giving credit to the original authors, each of whom was far more experienced than I.

I feel fortunate I experienced my brain injury during a period of time when technology and medicine met on the same page... embracing the human brain has, as many physicians note, "it's own unique way of healing." We can all have more hope, knowing brain issues previously believed to be incurable or irreversible can be vastly improved... just by knowing the brain has the capacity to repair itself, and generally improve how it functions.

I am not the person to speak from the medical or technical level, so the following information is based on the vast reading and research I completed, as I sought constantly to understand my injury. As I have noted before, there is a significant number of books available on the topic, and as you continue your journey, I encourage you to become a hungry reader. Enjoy other stories like my own—of people who have survived and now thrive sufficiently to share their experiences with others; enjoy the knowledge shared through online organizations and books by practitioners who provide the medical assistance necessary for optimum healing.

The first book that caught my eye was *Brainlash: Maximize Your Recovery From Mild Brain Injury* by Gail. L. Denton, Ph.D. Holding the book in my hand for the first time, I felt hope rise from deep within. How could I go wrong? The author was s both a psychotherapist and a brain injury survivor. Her passion for writing the book was to help her make sense of her own experience and to share what she learned along the way. If you look at my copy of the book, you will find many highlighted sections, and pages with the corners turned so I could quickly return to the places where Dr. Denton presented an understanding of the depth and breadth of the road ahead for if I choose to participate fully in the process of my recovery.

The author was able to speak from and education and a personal experience... about life issues and our "executive function," and about both our physical and emotional bodies. It was in her section, <u>Toolbox</u>, I learned of journaling. However, in retrospect, I believe the most impactful passage I read in her book was found on page 113; the header grabbed my heart and mind: <u>Declare New Life!</u> "All in all, declaring that you have a new life is a good idea. Wallowing in what used to be takes valuable time and energy you cannot spare. Discover for yourself that you are new, fresh and lovable. Get going!"

One of the first digital books I was able to read was Please Leave the Lights On: An Incredible Story of Recovering from Traumatic Brain Injury (Kindle Edition) by author, Harold Holder. His story, as a major business tycoon, was a prime example that no one "chooses" the challenges of TBI, or that so many different aspects of life are responsible for how our brains are afflicted; his was from a serious bout of pneumonia! A strong, successful man one day... the next taking one step at a time, committed to make progress and restore his health, his business and his life. Holder also used journaling as part of his journey; he proved for me that recovery is possible even in the midst of the most difficult times.

So that I don't extend this book's length beyond a comfortable, reasonable read, I am limiting the deeper "medical" coverage to the one area that most interested and fascinated me—neuroplasticity, which is the property of the brain that enables it to change and heal. I invite you to tap into the messages of many scientists, doctors and patients who have benefited from this discovery to achieve transformations previously believed inconceivable!

Did you know, for four hundred years, medicine and science purported the brain could not be changed and that people with limitations or disorders were destined to remain... unchanged? Remember the days when the brain was described as a computer with hardware that over time wore out. How unfortunate for my parents' generation to live in a time when preserving the brains of our senior population was seen as a waste of time!

Oh! The Journey | Bobbie R. Yeates

How grateful I am technology aided scientists in challenging the doctrine of the *unchanging brain*. Little did I know when my accident occurred in July, 2003, that in 2000 scientist, Eric Kandel, won the Nobel Prize in Physiology for his discovery that "mental activity is not only the product of the brain, but also a shaper of it." We no longer live in a time when we are told we can never get better; although we may be different as our neurons adjust the "circuitry," we no longer have to rely on temporary changes in the chemical balance of our brains. In fact, the brain's capacity "to form and re-form new connections, moment-by-moment," is the source of a unique kind of healing.

In your reading you will find hope... stories of people who were advised they, or their loved one, would never live a normal life—only to find them become fulfilled in life, independent and experiencing rich relationships.

In *The Brain That Changes Itself,* author Norman Doidge, noted maximum healing is brought about with alternative healing through the "use of energy—including light, sound, vibration, electricity, and motion." They are coupled with Eastern practices of the Chinese and Buddhist cultures long believed to be "far-fetched," but now known to be extremely effective. Gone are the days when the brain was believed to be stand-alone from the body; we now know "the brain is always linked to the body and, through the senses, to the world outside... the body and mind become partners in the healing of the brain, and because these approaches are so non-invasive, side effects are exceedingly rare."

I think what I truly enjoy about the neuroplasticity approach is it invites me to be actively involved... as a whole patient... in the care of my mind, body and brain. Like Hippocrates saw the body as the healer, I fully embrace working with my physician—and nature—to help my body activate its own healing... in concert with my brain. And as Dr. Santiago recently noted, I am a miracle and shouldn't be doing all I am doing today.

From chronic pain to...Parkinson's disease.

From Huntington's and Alzheimer's disease to... strokes and seizures

From light therapy... to yoga and body work

From martial arts... to speech therapy

From visualization... to multiple sclerosis

Therapies are being discovered and used to successfully transform all nature of brain problems.

I often failed at trying to explain my jumbled, noisy head! Dr. Doidge explained it all so clearly. The injury causes damage to neurons that then do not normally process tasks because they are dead! Others are alive but they are distressed and send out bad signals. It is this "noisy brain" activity that causes what is called "learned non-use" and causes those of us with injuries to think we are failing, or failures.

I found myself fascinated by Doidge's book; it was not difficult to understand, and it opened my mind to our actual potential to heal. My heart was filed with hope, as I read—page after page—of ideas for those of us who may have, at one time or another, felt we were totally out of options, short of just taking life on the chin and adapting as best we could.

Imagine my delight when I realized that at one point I was totally disheartened by the reality that my brain had been essentially rewired—only to discover in the words of the acclaimed Dr. Doidge, "It is entirely possible to revive the circuits by training a different part of the brain to take over the task." A change in my understanding of the process brought about significant change in my attitude about that "rewiring!"

Oh! The Journey | Bobbie R. Yeates

This book truly was—for me—about the discovery of how the human brain heals, and the refreshing reality that as the mind and body become partners in the process—miracles in healing can occur. The book is filled with stories of people who chose to participate in transforming their brains, and in the process were able to recover what they felt were lost parts of themselves and in many cases, uncover capacities they never knew existed. I encourage you to read this second book by an author who is truly vested in increasing awareness, and change the mindset of those who suffer any brain injury or disorder—reflecting the neuroplasticity abilities of a mind that participates in a unique restorative process.

You will read about how "non-use" of certain parts of our body and brain can be significantly "refurbished" when taken from a dormant state our minds chose—by our actions—to believe.

You will learn about noisy brains that don't generate enough strong signals, because the injury caused some neurons to die and cease to give off signals—for a period of time—not necessarily forever. The injury just messed with the "system" and neurons firing at the wrong or unusual rate, during which time the brain can't make the necessary fine distinctions for it to operate properly.

Light energy, therapy, lasers... a blind man learning to see and a devise that can reset the brain... how the brain balances itself and the impact of sound on the brain—each inspired me to read on, to absorb more, and increase my awareness and understanding of the possibilities for healing that yet lie ahead of me. As a layman, I can only encourage you to read this book and others that may offer a fine combination of understandable stories and enlightenment that will give you hope.

HELLO! ANYONE HOME?

If you would only recognize that life can be hard, things would be so much easier for you.

~ **Louis D. Brandeis** (1856-1941)
American judge.

HELLO!

Oh! The Journey | Bobbie R. Yeates

THE DAYS AND nights followed—one after another—as though absolutely nothing had happened in my life; as though absolutely nothing had changed. On the outside I was healed and for that I am grateful... there were no ugly scars to remind others around me of the day that forever changed my life, but I knew a "new" me had come to exist and I didn't quite know how to approach that new person; didn't quite know how to reach out and connect, or communicate with... or even for that matter, to understand and love. It was a new day, like me knocking on a neighbor's front door, shouting, "Hello! Anyone home?"

Writing to yourself about yourself may seem an oddity; it was a blessing to me—a journey of self-discovery and a renewed connection with all of life that surrounded me—in people, in nature, in relationships. I ask myself questions, such as "Who are you? and made bold statements like, "In the moment, you **are**!" And explored a curious world where I felt, "I am like a robot!" Each helped me walk along what was often a dark, cloudy, mist-colored path, and with each step, sought to re-discover Bobbie. Was she going to be who I always thought she was, or would I be surprised by who she was to become?

WHO ARE YOU?

YOU ARE UNIQUE.
In the whole world, there is only one you.

You are worth... everything.

There is only one person with your touch, your inner feelings, and your personal connection with your savior.

No one can take your place.

God created only one you—precious in His sight.

You have God's given gift of love—to care, to create, to grow, to give unconditionally.

If you believe in yourself it does not matter what happened yesterday—just what you choose to do today.

Nourish the seeds within you... celebrate you and start anew.

Give yourself a new beginning—today

You are you, and that is all you need to be.

You are here today—tomorrow is gone—so celebrate today with a new beginning, a new life, a new you.

IN THE MOMENT, YOU ARE

Seeing... life with new eyes.
Recapturing... the gift of now.
Recognizing... there is something EXTRAordinary happening in your life.

> ***Embracing...*** *this moment as you stop and look around and see the beauty surrounding you. It is everywhere and if you stay in the moment, you will discover what is right before your eyes.*
>
> ***Discovering...*** *that in whatever way* **the gift of now** *came your way, you are still surprised at the fullness available in each moment.*
>
> ***Feeling...*** *the joy of being in the moment*
>
> ***Making...*** *you life all you want it to be.*
>
> ***Opening...*** *the gift of the new you. Look inside and see the precious life within.*

I AM LIKE A ROBOT

I GET UP in the morning... go through the same routine of getting myself ready for the day.

Now... what are my plans?

First... I need to stay centered. I wonder, why doesn't anyone share their ideas with me? Why don't they ask my opinion?

That line of thinking causes me to consider whether others feel I have a chip on my shoulder, but I know the underlying cause is wondering where my brain has gone, and why I cannot remember.

I have come to realize our brains are indeed very fragile and need to handle them with care, and I busy myself with writing down numerous questions to reconnect with me...

> *Do you like yourself, Bobbie?*
> *Are you happy with your life?*
> *What would you like to change, and why?*
> *Why do I feel like I am being tested all the time?*

Oh! The Journey | Bobbie R. Yeates

THINGS ABOUT ME

LIFE IS NOT always kind; it sometimes forces us to face the truths that break us from our comfort zone. I don't recall exactly where this exercise began, but I took the suggestion to heart and started to reconnect with myself by truthfully documenting all the wonderful little quirks and traits that make me, Bobbie! It was a productive exercise, where—in those truths—I came to know just who was "home" and to love the person residing within.

I am impetuous.
I make decisions without thinking them through.
I impulse shop.
I am easily distracted.
I have difficulty concentrating in noisy places.
I forget what people tell me.
I easily lose and misplace items.
I have trouble concentrating on one thing—or holding a thought for very long.
I tire easily, mentally and physically—that fatigue worsens the pressure to think about or emotionally manage a situation.
I am overly sensitive to light, sound, motion and tense environments.
I have trouble following a map or directions to any location; I get turned around far too easily.
I lose track of time.

Oh! The Journey | Bobbie R. Yeates

I set priorities, get lost in other things... distracted, I get angry with myself because I have failed to fulfill my obligations.

When it comes to safety, I know I need to be more aware of my surroundings, pay attention and not be so vulnerable, gullible, or trusting.

I sometimes have a problem remembering where I put my purse, keys, glasses, etc.

I sometimes forget who I am calling—and why.

I do not sleep well most of the time.

I get overwhelmed too easily.

I am very restless; I lack patience.

I worry more than I should.

There is change in my sex drive.

I respond differently to lots of things and let many of them bother me.

I feel lost so often—like I can no longer be in control of my life.

I feel like I am on a roller coaster ride and that it will never end—up and down, around and around.

I get very emotional; feel distressed and shed a lot of tears.

I definitely have mood swings.

All in all—I feel frightened, angry, distressed, stressed and emotionally challenged about most things in my life.

I need an extra dose of courage—quite often.

I allow myself to follow the leader, instead of trying to be one.

Recognizing these traits helps to face them, learn to better deal with them and move forward toward better days.

Dreams

You are the one who has to decide,
Whether you do it or toss it aside.
You are the one to make up your mind,
To follow your dreams or leave them behind.
Whether you try for the goal that's far,
Or just be contented to stay where you are.
Reach out—believe in what you do,
It's your dream, it's all up to you.
What do you wish—to give it your best,
Or be the loser—who failed the test.
Your dreams grow stronger,
Each day you hold on a little longer.
Take the time to dream and plan,
And don't be discouraged by your fellow man.
Believe in dreams that challenge you!
It's up to you—what are you going to do?
Point your arrow at the star,
Take your aim, and there you are!

I AM A SURVIVOR
ARE YOU?

*We do not live to think, but,
on the contrary, we think in order that we may
succeed in surviving.*

~ Jose Ortega y Gasset (1883-1955)
Spanish philosopher.

Oh! The Journey | Bobbie R. Yeates

THERE WILL BE a pivotal moment in your life... one where you know, with unbridled certainty, you are a survivor! If I leave you with but one gem in *Oh! The Journey*, it will be that you find renewed hope that you will survive everything traumatic brain injury throws your way. My quest, however, is to bring you to that point of believing, and nudge you forward, one little inspired moment at a time... to surpass survival and begin to thrive!

SELF-TALK AND WORDS

WHY AM I writing, and why do I feel compelled to share with others? When you experience the life-changing event of a traumatic brain injury, you begin to realize how you are still able to take some of the memories of the past, reflect upon the possibilities of the future, and embrace one reality: the gift of life goes hand in hand with the gift of time.

My questions then become, "Why does the clock control your life? Are you comfortable with that outside control, or are you ready to make some changes?" Essentially, we may not understand many of the whys of our past:

WHY did this happen to me?
WHY was I allowed to live—granted a new life?
WHY am I being punished?

The why's seem never to stop; they churn and spin in our minds:

WHAT does the future hold for me?
WHAT do I have to live for?

Oh! The Journey | Bobbie R. Yeates

You may never fully understand the why, but to allow that to immobilize you... is a travesty! You cannot escape the reality you have been given time...

> **TIME** to reflect on your past and look forward to a future that although different than you had planned, may actually be far richer and more fulfilling—*if* you but open your heart to the possibilities.
>
> **TIME** to reflect on many beautiful memories no one can take from you; *if* those memories continue to add value and positive impact on your life today.
>
> **TIME** to let memories build a new future; *if* they are memories that make us smile, laugh, and really look forward to every tomorrow.

But... only if you courageously let go of the past!

Stop and think this through with me. If we have been given the innate ability to remember, should we not then seek to get rid of the "if only's" that keep us trapped in the past, and replace them with something more positive, such as "even though?" What if you took great care to rid your conversations of the "what ifs" and filled them with the hope that is more prevalent in an "even if?

I challenge you to take it one more step and cease the endless cycle of dwelling on the past using words like *shoulda, woulda, coulda*.

> *Some words do little more than place you in a state of allowing yesterday to take over today, resulting in little more than allowing your past to become a prison—a self-made prison in which we consciously choose to live.*

Memories can be beautiful, but there is great caution to make sure they to not prevent us from moving forward.

Oh! The Journey | Bobbie R. Yeates

WE CANNOT CHANGE *what has happened—not only is it not healthy, it is just not possible and to try to do so is an exercise in futility.*

WE CANNOT CHANGE *the past—but we can choose to change how it affects our future.*

Oh! The Journey | Bobbie R. Yeates

A Heart full of Love
Don't let the dark days trouble you,
Whatever trials life brings
Some day, just like the dove,
You'll find that you have wings
And a heart full of love.
Don't hurry and worry, frown and complain
Don't add to the clouds in the sky
As life's precious days may pass you by.
Don't be sad and blue
You know, being happy is up to you
Don't be tired and discouraged
And sad-hearted too.
For everyone is waiting for sunshine
And friendship from you
Take you smile with you
Wherever you go
Keep it bright… pass it along…
Always remember
You're where you belong.

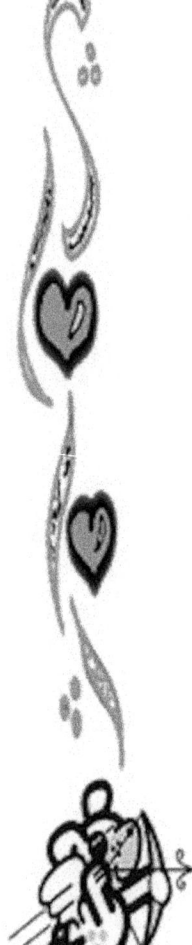

Oh! The Journey | Bobbie R. Yeates

MY OWN PAST is rich with speaking, writing poetry and sharing other motivational moments. Yes, they are my past, but they remain a positive part of me I cherish and want to re-enter into my future.

A serious accident changed my life, but I can choose to be encouraged to leapfrog from that experience to accept the gift of time I have been given. I am here today for a reason, and as I accept that gift, I take up the flame to share the message that, "Life is not a race; it is the beautiful gift of time."

> *TIME to count my blessings...*
> *TIME to accept the challenges of a bright, new future and look forward to them.*

As I write about challenges that accompany traumatic brain injury, I think back to a time before that accident and a poem I wrote. At the time I was so sure its message was intended for others; yet here I am today, wondering about the infinite wisdom and mysterious ways of our Creator. How is it that—at a time I am not capable of that creativity—the poem is available for me to "listen" to my own words and reflect upon them. There they are in a much shared poem, appropriately titled "Challenges," ready to nurture and nourish me.

Challenges

Life is a challenge… you are a challenge.
By accepting life, I challenge you to—
Enjoy today… Look forward to tomorrow.
Set goals, believe in yourself—
and believe in others.
Be thankful for success… but don't be afraid to fail.
Feel good about laughing,
but don't be afraid to cry.
Forgive those that have wronged you…
have faith.
Take time for yourself—but never forget a friend.
Work for what you believe in… make things happen. If you make mistakes learn from them.
Always give a smile,
for you may receive one in return.
Remember… God created only one you. Only one you to accept his challenge for life
And remember… "Tomorrow may never come, so live for today!"

- Bobbie Yeates

It is possible we need not learn how to live; but learn to remember...

If we can quit being afraid of slowing down and look at time as a gift to ourselves we can also believe there really will be many other days.

If we allow ourselves to indulge in having extra time, we can slow the speed at which we inadvertently attempt to live life.

I passionately repeat, "Life is not a race, nor is it a mere measure of time passing. It is the measuring of time that causes us so much stress."

To someone who suffers the impact of traumatic brain injury that stress can seem overwhelming when we are told, "Listen to your brain. It will tell you when it is time to rest!" However, what I have come to learn, and why I am compelled to share with you, is that a rested mind is open to acts of love, kindness, compassion, tenderness, patience and understanding. These are critical to the healing process, yet in our rush to do so, we fail to engage in one action that ensures we will, indeed, heal.

A Deep Dive

TODAY I AM frustrated enough about being unable to forgive certain things—and how it alters my personality—to do something about getting a few answers to my unending questions. The underlying pain that calls me to this deep dive was a recurring feeling of guilt for wanting to have the quantity and quality of support from my family that I am allowed to talk about the accident and the life I have lived since then. In many ways I feel like I have been forced to live in

Oh! The Journey | Bobbie R. Yeates

a bubble, intended to separate that I am today from the person I know previously existed.

I needed answers that were either not provided me by the physicians who treated me, or responses I had forgotten. The deep dive I needed was to thoroughly research medical information about the diagnosis and treatment of traumatic brain injury. I spent too much time listening to others tell me what I should be feeling, how I should be acting, and whether or not I should consider myself healed. I heard rumblings about perhaps clinging to a status that was no longer valid. Thus, I was compelled to discover for myself—and respond to many questions based on my *reality*—rather than the a*ssumptions* of others whose actions and comments came from a deep love for me, but did not necessarily take into account the reality that I lived with a re-wired brain!

I studied the things I felt; things that were true fact for me, and identified those I *experienced* more that I *felt,* after the length of time, would have been healed. Now keep in mind, I wanted to be done with this whole thing, so some people may question whether I was grasping at straws in my quest to find more answers, rather live the life I woke up to each day.

I certainly don't suggest you refuse—or fail to engage professional services—but if this is the first place you start your path to discovery, I hope you can recognize or refute symptoms you may experience. Keeping in mind how many differences there are among those who suffer from brain trauma—

> the actual **injury**,
> the **treatment** to which we may or may not have access,
> the **support system** we are afforded,
> basic **differences in our brains**, and
> what **part was injured**, and even our DNA.

Oh! The Journey | Bobbie R. Yeates

Each person will suffer different symptoms: some more; some less. The following are things I was actually able to recognize that caused my discomfort and suffering.

>***HEADACHES***, *dizziness and a general loss of balance sitting and standing.*
>
>***CHANGE IN SENSES****; taste and smell. For example for the first three years, I had to confirm with my family members whether I liked the taste of something, and after all these years my senses of smell and taste remains altered.*
>
>***DECREASED HEARING*** *in some instances; yet increased sensitivity to certain sounds and crowded, noisy environments.*
>
>***CHANGE IN VISION*** *that I believe is beyond what I would otherwise, normally experience, including double vision and sensitivity to bright lights.*
>
>***SLEEP DISTURBANCE****: difficulty falling asleep, waking up too early; mixed up sleeping cycles and never feeling fully rested.*
>
>***MEMORY LOSS****: extreme difficulty remembering people, conversations, places, events, instructions, appointments, telephone numbers and dates.*
>
>**THE WIND:** Although a rather interesting phenomenon, you may experience, as I continue to do so, that the wind plays havoc with you! It has never been kind to me. I can be fine one moment and with a gust of wind, ripping through Wyoming's sky, I suddenly have severe headaches, bloodshot eyes and general discomfort. I have learned I must pay attention to the wind; I don't know if it is just the change in barometric pressure... fortunately, after some research, at the encouragement of my editor, I was able to determine there is a direct link to the discomfort people suffering from TBI feel with changes in barometric pressure. Yes! I knew it wasn't just me!

CHANGED EXPERIENCES: ALL IS WELL

SOME DAYS I spend sorting out things that help me better manage traumatic brain injury. I know I have that goofy "re-wired" brain now, but that does not mean I must give in to how it has transformed my life.

> *Some things I can't change, some experiences changed me, but at the end of the day, I know all is well.*

Have you ever wondered whether the clock controls your life? It is something that has bothered me since the accident. I used to have it "all together" but now I seem not to have enough time to get things done. I set an agenda for every day and promise myself I will not schedule too many things into one day.

Focus, Bobbie! One project! Finish one project before you move on to another.

I feel like I am running out of time, but somehow in the mix of the day discover I have traveled many different directions, and not completed even one project. What is wrong with me? I find it nearly nighttime and I am tired—no, let's call it what it really is—I am exhausted! I really just want to go to sleep. There is always another day. Or is there?

Overall, however, this has given me the ability to see happiness at a different level. It is certainly taken many ups and downs to realize the importance of everyday things... **every one in my life.**

Oh! The Journey | Bobbie R. Yeates

Some days are actually better than others as I allow myself not to worry about clocks and schedules and getting projects done. ***I focus only on the simple joys.***

Awakening to the smell of coffee brewing, a big smile bursts from me and I give excited greetings to another day.

Six O'clock High

It is six in the morning
The sun barely up
As I walk a steady pace
Knowing yesterday's gone,
And today's just beginning
"Oh! How I look forward to tomorrow.
Each day brings a new challenge
New goals to be set
And goals to reach
I can't stop reaching,
For if I do
My tomorrows will end

Oh! The Journey | Bobbie R. Yeates

***It isn't the big pleasures that count the most;
it's making a great deal of the little ones.***

What a life lesson this has been! We can, indeed, gather simple pleasures from the smallest things, and in so doing, find the most precious things in our lives are within hand's reach—all we must do is reach out! When I think about reaching out, I am reminded that all important truths are within our reach, and the best and most beautiful of them cannot be seen or touched, as Helen Keller notes, "... they must be felt with the heart." These precious things are "at hand" and the wise ones will gather them up, be grateful and look forward to what comes tomorrow.

Even the important truths in life are simple; in life, most good things come to us unexpectedly. As we journey along our path and we are open they will come in the form of kindness and love. As a child, I don't know if you remember finding pennies on the ground. Were you taught to put the penny in your shoe for good luck, or did you learn that if you found it heads up you were to pass it on to the first person you see? If you were looking for good luck, did that represent things to you, or perhaps the kind of perpetual happiness that comes in the form of good health and wonderful memories?

I BELIEVE—Do You?

Believe that life is worth living and your belief will help create the fact.

~ William James (1842-1910)
American philosopher.

Oh! The Journey | Bobbie R. Yeates

LIFE HAS SO many ups and down; the downs being very challenging and the ups oh, so easy. No matter, we learn from life... and the important thing is to get started!

Having walked a difficult path—suffering from traumatic brain injury—I have learned in order to get beyond the thought of just surviving—the path to thriving in life calls for an added breath of courage, an extra dose of being optimistic... each of which serves to keep you going day-by-day, step-by-step.

> *How did I manage to get beyond the struggle, the pain, the confusion, the doubt? I had to take time to heal; take time to wrap myself in the things I recognized brought soothing to my body, mind, heart and soul.*

I woke up many days with nothing more than my innate belief in the spirit of the Holy Ghost; in our most loving, gracious father. I knew within that belief I could make it through one more day—take one more step—and face head on whatever came my way. Granted, I had human questions about the why, however, the Lord remained on my mind when I certainly could not understand why I was hurt; I came to accept I may have to struggle with the brain injury, but I was still here! I have much to fulfill—in my duties here on earth—and some how, some way, I am to serve others... through the very things I was to experience. My mind often rambled with questions, and then crystal clear revelations like the following came, as I allowed the thoughts and feelings to easily flow to the pages of my journals.

Always remember, no matter what is going on in your life... it is your responsibility to choose how to respond. Reacting just doesn't get it!

I now know how I have no responsibility to please others or to be everything to everyone. I do not have to do it all; to be it all.

Oh! The Journey | Bobbie R. Yeates

I can rest peacefully in the reality that I am one of a kind—uniquely me—and it is ok to love the different me enough to be ok with this new person.

My career has been wrapped in the beauty industry, but my experience with traumatic brain injury helped me to expand my perspective beyond the external. I came to embrace beauty as being how you invite people into your life and heart. It is when you are authentic and vulnerable... when you laugh or cry with your whole being.

**Beauty has been redefined in my mind...
it is seen through the eyes of courage, energy,
joy, and grace.
Beauty is you—just the way you are.**

Know in your heart that change is what provides you the choice to be yourself, and the opportunity to make your life everything you want it to be.

LOOKING FORWARD

I AWOKE THIS morning with a steady stream of thoughts about how to look ahead and leave all the pain of yesterday behind. I thought you would enjoy them. I don't know that there is any rhyme or reason to them; I only know they were part of my morning awareness.

> *Squeeze a stone in your hand.*
> *Wiggle my toes.*
> *Open my eyes and close them, open them again.*
> *Moan and groan, ah, smell that coffee!*

Once I had connected with those thoughts, the real message came shortly thereafter.

See life as a journey, not a destination, which means we need not have such a deep preoccupation with future goals, but willing to be conscious of our progress, and fully open to the lessons and life transformation that often accompany us in the twists and turns in life.

THE SCATTERED MIND

I CAN'T SEEM to turn off my brain—one thing after another is crossing its terrain, each quickly changing to another, and yet another.

There have been so many nights sleep has eluded me, and sometimes I have been grateful for that time to figure out something important that has been on my mind. The sleeplessness actually has brought clarity about why noise and a competitive environment messes with my brain. I am pleased to finally understand why some days I feel better than others. I can embrace that I can be obsessive about things, but not selfish; and how much healthier an environment I create for myself when I focus on things I know about rather than chasing after things about which I have such little awareness.

Oh! The Journey | Bobbie R. Yeates

TRUTHS AND BELIEFS···

I GREW UP in the days of hearing words of wisdom from my elders, whom I often wondered whether they learned them from Ben Franklin! You know the feeling; the phrases were so old fashioned you just knew one of the sages of life actually scribed them. Funny how life comes round full circle, and suddenly those things you pushed aside have some real meaning—offering a small amount of peace and solace on a gray day.

To live simply is to live well; to eat simply is to live longer.

The foolish man seeks happiness in the future; the wise man grows it under his feet.

Beauty of style and harmony and grace and good intentions depend on simplicity.

Gratitude unlocks the fullness of life; it turns what we have into enough—and more.

Simplicity is like the key to seeing things clearly and openly.

He is richest who is content with the least.

Respect yourself and others will respect you.

Rise and shine; share your love and light.

Search your inner-self and discover new wisdom.

Life is a gift; enjoy it and encourage others to do the same.

Relax and do all you can to see the beauty in our world.

Open your heart and soul to more love every day.

As you rise each day, whatever you are guided to do—do it and it will be a success.

Oh! The Journey | Bobbie R. Yeates

All you need for happiness in life is love, belief and wisdom.

If you don't remember the day... remember the moment.

Let riches not consist in the extent of your possessions, but in how few your wants.

Happiness is not a destination... it is found along the way in simple pleasures and in acts of love and kindness.

Always have something beautiful in sight; even if it is just a sunrise of another day.

MOMENTS OF TRUTH

All truths are easy to understand once they are discovered; the point is to discover them.

~ Galileo Galilei (1564-1642)
Italian scientist.

BODY IMAGE

MY BODY CHEMISTRY is out of balance and my weight is up. I have other physical concerns and all I can hear is my brain proclaiming, *Get a sticky note!*

Later, I understood that brain command. I needed the sticky note to leave a note to myself. "Bobbie, think enthusiasm and self esteem! Love yourself enough to risk sharing your inner most passion." This was but a part of what I came to call my "fuzzy brain" days. They were interesting days in which I was able to find strength and courage and know I would trudge forward, doing what I could under whatever circumstances came my way.

A good brain day is a wonderful thing!
Soak it up; remember it and write it down!

THE GIFT OF AWARENESS

ULTIMATELY, WHAT WE pay attention to is often a clue to how we really want to spend our time. In this present moment I am grateful for the opportunity to use something as discomforting as traumatic brain injury as a Launchpad for finding my life's purpose. This Old English prayer says much!

TAKE TIME to work; it is the price of success.

TAKE TIME to think; it is the source of power.

Oh! The Journey | Bobbie R. Yeates

TAKE TIME to play, it is the secret of perpetual youth.

TAKE TIME to read; it is the foundation of wisdom.

TAKE TIME to be friendly; it is the road to happiness.

TAKE TIME to dream; it is like hitching your wagon to a star.

TAKE TIME to laugh and be loved; it is the privilege of the gods.

TAKE TIME to look around; it is too short a day to be selfish.

TAKE TIME to laugh; it is the music of the soul.

FAMILY

BRAIN INJURY HAS an undetermined period of recovery, making the journey even more traumatic. It seems like we can better manage things when there is a finite amount of ourselves to which we have to commit; the unknown does little more than drain us. It brings up feelings that may well not be valid, coming from bruised egos and other emotional tailings attached to our day-to-day existence in a vastly changed world. The following are some of the emotions, which I experienced following the accident and know I would now look more kindly on the events that pushed all my buttons back then.

I hurt so deeply; I feel my husband speaks down to me and feel I am omitted from many conversations. It is with some frequency I need to go away so my family won't have to deal with me. But then... I get angry when I think of the accident—why it happened, the why me, and the pervading question of why I always feel on the defensive.

Oh! The Journey | Bobbie R. Yeates

Within a year of the accident, my brain surgery, returning home, acting the part, and working very hard at looking like my old self, I feel I have achieved a great deal. Yet, **I am confused and disillusioned with life***... I am no longer comfortable in my own skin, mostly because I look the part but know the inside is not in concert with the blessing I had of not being scarred for life.*

Little things tear at me*; I feel freakish and no longer the person I once was. I have no taste buds or a "smeller" that works! Although there is kindness in the actions of others, I hate that I have to be told I like something I have completely forgotten I enjoyed. I spend much of my time watching others around me—no one knows, but I am the official observer!*

I was never a whiner! Now I question that perhaps I am! I just want so much to feel complete again but have to accept my improvements will continue for the rest of my life. "Face it," I tell myself, "You have been injured... and **that** *is your reality!" Don't let yourself get caught in the swirling back hole of believing your family feels you use the injury as a crutch! I have to get beyond feeling violated some how when I know they don't want me to discuss my situation or if given their preference... think about it. It will never be over. I cannot just "let it go!" Because I am not one to shed precious tears, I am willing, however, to get on with the future that lies before me, but steadfastly defy anyone to make me feel guilty or ask me why—ever again."*

FATIGUE

TODAY I FELT the effects of an unannounced emotional fatigue. Like a dark English mist it crept silently around until it fully surrounded me. I associated it with a degree of stress I was feeling, but the effect was a seriously diminished sense of self-esteem that left me feeling fragile.

I am fragile; should I be treated gently at all times?

My energy is fragile.

My emotions and self-esteem are fragile.

Almost anything can set me off and flame my temper in a flash.

Note to self: *Bobbie, learn to love these challenging moments, see them as a gift in this journey, and give your self permission to embrace all the elements of healing tied to this invisible visitor.*

Note to self: *Bobbie, you have what it takes to learn how to accept the changes you continue to experience.*

LOVE IS...

THERE IS AN extraordinary thing we call love... a feeling of depth, delight and ecstasy. It is often the one thing that keeps our hearts filled with hope. Don't discount its power; don't falter as you allow your journey to take you in its direction.

> *LOVE is the magician, the enchanter, and the power that changes worthless things to joy.*
> *LOVE fills the world with melody; treasure what you receive above all else.*
> *LOVE is life; do all things with love.*
> *LOVE is the river of life in this world; with love your life will vibrate with warmth and meaning.*

Search for love; we have learned to love and that even in hardship, love will shine through.

SEE DYING AS A GIFT

TO SEE DYING as a gift diminishes the pain in which you view it. American poet, Emily Dickinson is noted to have said, *Dying is a wild night and a new road. If we consider living forever, we might actually feel trapped in our lives.* Alternatively, when looking at death as a homecoming, we recognize that pivotal moment where the soul is reunited with its source. I want not to appear morbid, nor do I want you to imagine I was ever on the verge of calling life quits. No! I want only to reference the moment when I realized I am ever so grateful I survived my accident, and even though my journey was complicated by that event, it did open a new road for me. I never felt "trapped" in my life before traumatic brain injury, and for that I feel blessed; however, that pivotal moment did occur when I fully embraced my soul was united with its source, as you will see in my "three AM thoughts" and "be inspired by clouds!"

THREE AM THOUGHTS

I AM OFTEN awakened at 3 AM; awakened with my brain flooded with a fresh thought I have to figure out how to help with my healing, or help me make it through the next day.

> **NEVER STOP** learning... about your self, other people and the world at large. Learning ensures we remain flexible and responsive and able to deal with whatever happens to us as we effect the changes we seek.

> **MEET YOUR** angel... close your eyes and imagine yourself at the edge of a dark forest. Ahead of you is a path; you follow the path, which winds into the heart of the forest. Eventually, you come to a clearing where there is a temple. A bright white light is emanating from the doorway. As you enter the temple, you see a beautiful angel; a being of light. The angel holds its arms open for an embrace. In that moment of knowingness, you are acutely aware the angel knows and understands everything about you and your life.

> *This angel is the companion sent so share my journey and guide my life. I feel confident this companion will always be*

near—prepared to give me everything I may need—from unconditional love to much needed support. I feel compelled to hide this angel from the rest of the world so I keep a secret place where I go... knowing my angel will be there to greet me.

A MESSAGE OF FAITH

Faith consists in believing when it is beyond the power of reason to believe.

~ **Voltaire** (1694-1778)
French Writer

Oh! The Journey | Bobbie R. Yeates

SO MANY WHYS

*A*M I HAVING *a heart attack? This seizure is not normal, I am afraid, what do I do? Why is this happening?* The thoughts rushed through my fragile mind like the winds of a tornado; twisting, turning, tearing me apart. I found the courage to drive myself to the hospital, being ever so fearful of bothering anyone else. As I sat in the hospital parking lot, I felt lost and alone, taking deep breaths to quiet my crying, but never being able to dispel the one thing in my mind, "Why?" How desperately I needed the medical attention, but I was frozen in place, totally at the mercy of a disquieted mind that flooded me with what, at the time, I felt were totally *rational* thoughts.

You cannot afford this, Bobbie

You are just feeling sorry for yourself. Why don't you just die so everyone else can get on with their lives without bothering and worrying about you?

The mean spirit that had come to reside with me since the accident spoke loud and clear. "Are you having fun yet, Bobbie?"

My only response was a faltering voice that whispered, "Why, God? Why this? Why me?"

The pain in my head eased somewhat, and I remember thinking, again—what I thought was rational—*Learn to deal with it, Bobbie, this and so many other things, like the uproar you know you have created with Garth! What next?*

Oh! The Journey / Bobbie R. Yeates

My mind wanders to a problem I subconsciously find much more looming than the attack that brought me to sitting in the hospital parking lot—Garth. Again, that violent storm of fear-filled, confusing thoughts that cripple me—prevent me from any type of action at all.

Bobbie, I chide myself, you know Garth likes to come home and rest, not having you waiting with a honey-do-list or some new idea you have. You know these things make him not even want to come home; you have a problem. How are you going to fix it?

In my more lucid moments, I came to discover I experienced problems with many people whom I cherished. Visiting with Heather, I discovered how disappointed in me she was. What clouded my mind again, however, was my memory of her telling me I lie to her. In my fear and concern, I think this over: *I know I have never intentionally lied to her. I just know it! What am I doing that make my responses to her appear to be lies? How can I fix that? I don't know how to fix what I don't understand. I know it must have something to do with how I express myself, but what is the loss in brain function that causes nothing to come out right? How-do-I-fix-it?*

At some point, I must have had a bad incident at the hotel. I am not clear of the exact event. I just know it brought me to another flood of emotions that controlled me far more than I ever could. *I feel discriminated against. I am angry and my defense mechanism supports me and tells me I have done everything in my power and ability to improve the hotel—not just its looks but absolutely everything about it—whatever it takes to make sure travelers want to come back. I haven't tried to interfere with the business side of things, but I am an owner and what are my rights?* **Indignant!** *Now there is a word, Bobbie. This is how you really feel when you are denied the use of the Visa card or petty cash. This is why you are angry when* *business partners choose not to share anything that goes on with the hotel. Your big why is certainly as justified as your anger and frustration.*

Around and around I go. There is this dance that seems to occur in my mind. I liken it to a fluid movement of life where my brain swirls things around and around as it dips and dives with the very things that disrupt me emotionally. My questions? They are rather like a huge crowd of polished performers who know exactly what they are doing, but the answers that seem never to come are more like the stifled, shy kid who stands on the side line at a high school dance asking "Why not me?"

Once so confident that life is a gift, I am forced to embrace the reality: Life is different—does it, in this form, remain a gift?

Fast Forward Three Years

It is 2006 and from what I have been told, and what I have read, there should be some serious progress in my recovery and healing from traumatic brain injury and I have found the courage to believe it is time I start to write about my experience. Someone, somewhere, needs to hear my story; it will change their lives—forever for the better. The following are the feelings I experienced on February 14th; a day I will always remember.

Garth is in Dubois working, and my love for him overflows; I am grateful for the "us" and I want the day to be special—special above and beyond it being Valentine's Day! What a joy to shop for the things I know he will enjoy: that new microwave all our friends are talking about, and an oven with a rotisserie in it. I am so excited!

Unfortunately, the day did not end as I planned. It took virtually no time for me to hear the hurtful message that he wouldn't use it as he questioned why I even purchased it... and the final kicker, "I don't like change!" Now, at some other point in our lives, I may have kept a tight cap on having my happy bubble burst, but not this time! The new Bobbie that was surfacing from the accident and the brain injury had something to say. I don't know who was more surprised, Garth or me, at the bold explosion of words I spew forth, but spew I did!

"It's my house, too, and I do like change! I am a compulsive person (now) and I like to change things too often, and oh, yes, I am a clean freak. I also don't think the new me can ever understand why our home and my needs and wants always come last!"

Apparently the dance of drama that played out in my brain did not stop on that day, nor for several days after. Fast forward; and my memories run, flowing like a river flooding, about what the new me decided to do next and the thoughts associated with that decision.

What a day you've had, Bobbie!

I know this is true for everyone, but I think it may be more strongly felt by those of us who suffer TBI; not all days start off as we expect them when we wake up! I needed Garth for something that at the time was very important to me; he happened to be at the popular Ron Thon wrestling tournament but made me very aware he was not going to be there for me and wasn't in the frame of mind or in the time or place for any of my "Honey-do's." To make matters worse, I reached out to Heather shortly thereafter, and she also made me feel I was an

Oh! The Journey | Bobbie R. Yeates

imposition. *That's it!* I thought. *I am going to stop being a burden to my family. They don't deserve this; I need to row my own boat and let their lives, at least, resume to the normal they used to know.*

It all seemed so simple; I would take a trip on my own. It didn't take much for me to get up, pack what I felt was needed, make sure everything in the house was clean, and head south to see Aunt Wilma.

I can handle this! Pick up discount cards from the hotel—check. Make sure the roads are passable with the snow—check. The car is all winterized and warm—check!

Even though I didn't think to check the temperature, I had all the faith in the world I could make it from Point A to Point B! Unfortunately, real life happens around all our planning. Wyoming's winter snows can be deadly and in my lack of rational thinking, I took the wrong road—going to Rawlins over Sand Draw—not Rock Springs over South Pass. Oh, well!

Actually, I was trying to figure out exactly where I was going so I could see my daughter, Maygen, in Pocatello, by way of Salt Lake, on my way to Auntie Wim's in Peoria, Arizona! *What a journey; I can figure this one out without much problem!*

I hate getting lost!

Garth, the good husband that he is, called to talk me into coming home, but I had already thought it through in my mind to tell him, "No!" if he did call and ask me, so I kept on trucking through that snow. By the time I arrived at Little America, I decided to turn around and return to Rock Springs to spend the night rather than fight with the white-out.

Little girl lost? She was scared to death, but not about to admit it!

Oh! The Journey | Bobbie R. Yeates

Garth called again when I was on the road and helped me find my way to the Quality Inn in Rock Springs and I ended my day thinking, *I am here; all is well. I can figure it all out tomorrow. I don't need to know what I am going to do right now; I am too tired to care. Oh! Thank you, Lord, for getting me here safely.*

Where we love is home — home that our feet may leave, but not our hearts.

~ Oliver Wendell Holmes, Sr.

AS MY STORY unfolded, I found my way home again, but did not really figure things out in my mind. My heart was so filled with love for my family and a desire to never cause hurt feelings or commotion in our lives, but I just didn't know what to do. The only recourse, in that present moment was to sit back, review the events of the past few days and see what surfaced in that battle of wills between my heart and my mind.

Hello again, Bobbie! You know your mind is mixed up, but be gentle with yourself; there is a lot to take in. Look at how much happened in so short a time frame. You know your primary objective was to take that trip just to prove to yourself (and others) you could be responsible.

Unfortunately, my ultimate achievement was frightening my family and friends... and me too! I almost giggled with the thought the one major revelation for me was, *I don't like traveling alone!*

Oh! The Journey | Bobbie R. Yeates

In the midst of all my reviewing the battle that was going on inside me, my fervent prayer was that Garth and I could find a way to figure this out and carry on with our lives—together. In my rational moments it was not difficult to connect with how my constant requests on Garth are a burden to him; nor was it impossible to make the assessment of how much I should be able to do for myself. The real cross to bear, however, was knowing if I could put "us" back together again it would require my willingness to turn the other cheek—whether I felt wrong(ed) or right.

I look around my home, trying to feel embraced by surroundings that should support me; support my journey to healing... to discovering and accepting this new person who evolved from the fire pit of brain trauma—and I wonder why I should have to feel guilty for wanting our lives back together and wanting our home completed. Who was the woman who was willing to wait 32 years to have the outside of her home finished? Where did that person go who never allowed her interests, wants or needs to supersede those of her family? Why is it necessary for me to validate how hard I have worked all my life, knowing my needs never reached the top of anyone else's list?

Stepping back from the thoughts that filtered through my tortured mind, I felt as though I was begging it to look at the multitude of other things I knew to be true—seeking to balance out the pain with some other reality—not feeling sorry for myself, just wondering what it's all about..

Garth and I have always worked together as a team.
Our marriage has never been one-sided; we each applied ourselves 100%.
All that we accomplished—especially the things that astonished those around us—were done in absolute tandem

as we shared the experience of achievement and pride as a family.

A lack of self-esteem and confidence are natural by-products of a brain injury, but I never realized how quickly it could be stripped, nor what havoc it would wreak in an otherwise strong and happy marriage. I am just grateful we are not of the statistic where a divorce rate up to 78% is reported in marriages impacted by traumatic brain injury. I guess I took for granted the confidence I had gained; confidence that had its very foundation in what I brought to our marriage union. I took for granted my independence and self-sufficiency, never considering how I would respond to borrowing money from Garth. Although he says the household money is ours, my confidence suffers mightily at having to "ask" him for it.

In the midst of all this personal assessment, I come face to face with another reality: I have no previous real association with or understanding of the concept of long-term or short-term memory. Imagine my shame and how it bruised my ego when I had to ask for an explanation of what I was dealing with. There was a glimmer of hope in the answer I received.

I was actually injured in the accident far worse than my family or I realized. I left the hospital too soon; I didn't have the therapy I probably needed in the worst way, and I was not clear on the reality that with this type of injury, partly because of its being relatively invisible, each day would bring something new for me to experience.

Whether it was good or bad was not my call, how discomforting it might be was not within my control, and having no one I was comfortable sharing it with... was the greatest pain of all.

The pain in my head is incredible! In my intense desire to shield everyone from my struggles, I call on every reserve I

Oh! The Journey | Bobbie R. Yeates

have to not scream. How do I even begin to explain something I don't understand and can't really define? I just want it to go away.

I don't try to fool myself. I know those who love me prayed I would awaken from those six long days of medically induced coma and be the Bobbie they knew and loved. I don't know if they will find the capacity to accept the realities of traumatic brain injuries. I certainly know I want to be accepted for who I am—now—what I have become, and experience life and love as I once knew it.

I have accepted I have changed; that was not my choice, but it is my reality. I have also accepted I may be something more, and someone better in that difference.

When I took my little trip a few days ago I wanted to be with Auntie Wilma because I feel comfortable with her! I just felt this overwhelming need to finally talk... and talk and talk and talk. I was almost afraid the floodgates would open and I'd be unable to close them down, but I knew the depth of my need. My real need was to talk to Garth, without thinking I was imposing or interrupting a meeting or writing up a bid.

It is interesting how the recriminations slip right in there. The questions of how God has allowed this, or what He has in mind to turn it into something good ran rampant in my mind. I continued to question where I might have failed, and frustrated with the times when I have to put on a happy face and pretend that life is fine; that I did not come away from the accident unscathed.

When do I get to quit all this painful pretending? We have an anniversary coming up in a few days; how do I get myself together so all that surfaces is the love I know I feel? How do I keep this brain in check?

Oh! The Journey | Bobbie R. Yeates

I surprised myself and made it through the weekend. I am beyond grateful our anniversary was wonderful. I don't want to sort out whether the smile in my heart and on my face was real or pretend. It went well and for that I am grateful. There were other issues and conversations, but because other things had gone so well, even the idea of allowing Garth to be the ultimate decision-maker did little to distract or disrupt my happiness. I also knowing we actually came away feeling each passing day was another step toward jumping another brain trauma hurdle — together.

Hello, world! I have decided to write a book. Have I talked about this before? I don't know that I recall. I am clear one day; the lights are dim and a misty cloud obscures my thoughts the next. This journey has been filled with far more pain than discovery, but as I feel the healing, my focus is more on helping others than myself. I actually recall how not so very long ago I was terrified at the idea of helping another person through this journey when I felt incapable of breaking through myself!

Life is cruel sometimes; it goes on with or without you being on board! My writing efforts were up one day; down the next. I wrote of significantly insignificant activities like booking trips for Garth and Maygen and I. I also wrote of the inspiration to write, whether I dared create an outline or allow it to be like my recovery — a complex maze I followed — at times trusting with blind faith I would stay on the right path.

The greatest inspired moment may well have been the decision to write of good things during a very bad time in my life.

I guess I will just sleep on it! Each day can be a miracle or a mystery. I know we are not to live life with the attitude of being happy when something specific happens, but my anger and prevailing sadness are diminished when I think about the pain in my head being gone. Having to leave dinner gatherings

Oh! The Journey | Bobbie R. Yeates

when I feel strange, experience dizziness or have headaches is not my cup of tea. Having to feel the pressure of writing about my recovery does not necessarily make the idea of writing a pleasant one.

Regardless the craziness of this injury, I remain grateful for so many things in life. What if I just start all this journaling from the beginning and focus on that gratitude? Is it important that it helps others; can I better navigate that confusing, overwhelming maze if my attention stays on my own recovery for a while longer?

I had the opportunity to sit down and write out "why I write" and found it both revealing and healing.

I enjoy sharing my feelings and experiences with others.

Writing is a release for me; I can unwind when I write.

I feel I have a lot to share.

I want people to know the impact of traumatic brain injuries not only on those of us who were injured, but everyone whose lives touch ours.

I want to be a well-known author. I can dream big, can't I and think of it providing a lot of benefit to readers on a very wide scale?

Motivation is my main purpose in writing.

Revenue that allows me the privilege of self-sufficiency and generosity to others would be nice, too.

Fashion is important to me. Ok! Where did that come from?

DAILY COMMUNICATION···

I HAVE SO much to say! We've all made negative choices in the past, yet this does not mean we are bad people, nor are we stuck with those choices. We can always choose to let go of old judgments. How do I manage this?

Daily I give thanks for life, and when I do, I find life says, "You are welcome!"

This is a new day! This is what I tell myself as I communicate with my creator. Let me take back the power you once gave me. I think I am ready to start—simply by loving and accepting myself unconditionally, as you have.

Everyday I listen for one new idea that will improve the quality of my life, and I realize my thoughts and desires may change on a daily basis; they continue wandering around in my "attic world" wondering which are right—and which are wrong.

BE INSPIRED BY CLOUDS

THOUGHTS TO REMEMBER... the sky does not impede the clouds in their flight! Meditate on this though for a while; allow your thoughts, like clouds, to drift across the surface of your mind, without trying to push them away or hold onto them.

Oh! The Journey | Bobbie R. Yeates

BEWARE

WE MUST ALWAYS take on the personal responsibility to beware of things that might further damage our already modified brains, and let me tell you... that is no easy job! Over the years I have had many occasions when life in general put me in a position I hadn't deemed dangerous, but the end result turned out to be something that threw me—and my injured brain—for yet another loop!

I opened the freezer on the porch to get something out, and who would believe it, but the heater on the top had shifted forward and came crashing down on... my head! It knocked me out, of course, and when I came to I felt the blood. I quickly got myself up and ran to Garth's Man Cave and the next thing I knew, we were on our way to the emergency room. Would you believe it? A two inch cut that was quickly patched up, but then came the tests to make sure I would be fine, and leaving me with a thought that seemed to be cropping up more and more lately, Life goes on, Bobbie!

Oh, and how dangerous would you think golfing would be? Here I am, it is a beautiful day and I am on a sand trap trying to hit my ball out (don't you hate it when your ball lands there?) and the next thing I know, I am lying in a crumpled position, holding onto my club for dear life and my friend's voice, coming from a far distance, "Bobbie, are you ok?" After a couple attempts to get my attention, she came over, and sure enough—I-was-not-ok! Apparently I had a seizure—another issue to deal with—and although I thought I might be ok, I decided it would be better to have her take me home, where

Heather and Garth could take over. Well... another trip to the emergency room.

There have been so many times when I have experienced those intuitive moments, thinking there was something of which I should be more acutely aware, but I didn't listen to my own warnings. I look back and think of many times I was aware... the warning bells clanking in my head, telling me to pay attention, or balance myself. The times I did not heed those warnings resulted in a consequence I may have been able to avoid.

Medications are another example of listening to your body when it tells you to beware! Your physician can only do the best he knows in prescribing what you need for pain, reduced anxiety, or what ever need you have; you have to watch what they do to you and if there is a red flag of any kind, share that information so you don't experience discomfort or some long-term damage from their use. Talk with your physician; ask questions and understand why you are being prescribed a particular medication, what to expect, and what long–term effects they may have on your body.

What is my caution to you? Take time to listen to yourself. Understand who you are, know yourself and how your body responds to certain things, and respect your intuition when it reaches out to protect you.

THE HEALING JOURNAL

I'm touched by the idea that when we do things that are useful and helpful—collecting these shards of spirituality - that we may be helping to bring about a healing.

~ Leonard Nimoy (1913-2015)
American Actor

Oh! The Journey | Bobbie R. Yeates

JOURNALING IS A great way to support the work you are doing. When I first started documenting my experiences I just wrote short little notes, as you will see throughout *Oh! The Journey*. Not only is it a natural and good place to start, it is an easier process to document or translate the sequence of your experiences, which can otherwise be burdensome, far too often leaving the consequences unspoken, locked up inside, or waiting for just the right moment to raise their nasty heads in more fear, anger, frustration, and overwhelm.

Little did I know there would be over seven million references to establishing goals, as related to establishing goals! Categorically, however (even though I did not read that many!) the objectives of all research was to determine the impact of occupational therapy in helping persons with traumatic brain injury achieve self-identified goals that would consistently take them from Point A to Point B in their daily lives. I did not have the privilege of this therapy; however, I do feel the steps I took, based on conversations with my physicians and the material gathered in my reading, support the benefit of setting goals on which I was able to focus and toward which I could remain motivated.

I have always been a "big dreamer!" I am confident I will always be, and believe they have played a big part in my staying the path... and that my journaling helped stimulate the awareness and the desires. As you read the next section about my days... well journaled, if you are still hesitant to put pen to paper, let me encourage you with the fact that you would not be reading my message today had I not found a way to document and share my journey. Furthermore, whether you have a story to share with others will only be discovered if—and when—you work to discover yourself through the magical words that sometime flow out—in unexpected moments; in uncommon hours!

A Day Well-Journaled

JOURNALING TAKES ON many tones and forms. When I first decided to write *Oh! The Journey*, I found sticky notes, note pads, journals, sheets of paper—you name it, I used it to jot down what I was feeling on any given day. I found them in dresser drawers, on my nightstand, and hidden in the pages of books I read... essentially everywhere! The following represent some of those spur of the moment thoughts quickly penciled on a free piece of paper lying in a much-needed place, at a much-needed time.

OUR FRIEND... MIND AND SPIRIT.

A tree, flourishing and growing in all weather and conditions.

Your wounds, like the knots and twisted branches bearing testament to life's struggles.

It is the imperfections of these sometimes giant beings that the true beauty lies; the source of uniqueness and strength.

The vast blue sky above—look—it is without limits, without boundaries; yet fully embracing the world.

OH! THE JOURNEY

Don't you see... the sun's journey, starting with a glimmering dawn, passes noon, then ends with a glorious sunset.

An apt metaphor for our human lives, this image serves as a reminder of the beauty and value of all stages of life and the eternal cycle of renewal.

Visualize your star—a point of light in the center of your head, just above your eyes. According to some eastern traditions, this is known as the "third eye," and represents the seat of intuition. Feel your star radiating energy, and whenever you require strength or inspiration, call it to mind and allow it to quiet you.

Can't seem to turn my brain off—one thing on my mind— and then it quickly switches to yet another. I call this my "no-sleep" time and I just recognized something important... too much noise and commotion really messes with my brain. I also realized how some days I am just naturally better than others, and that occurs when I work on things I am comfortable with and not obsess over things I think I should know about, but do not.

I seem to go in cycles; being ok with the status quo and struggling to figure out who I am. I keep trying to figure out why I should feel guilty for trying to understand this crazy new rewired brain and needing to talk about all these things with my family.

DEAR DIARY

I FOUND MY peace many times, turning to my journal with an almost simple, child-like approach to the private moments of communicating with my Diary, such as the following entries.

Dear diary—my friend,

There is so much to write about. I am on such an emotional roller coaster; I cannot seem to stay focused on a single thing. Why does my mind jump around continually? I have serious doubts I actually finish a thought or idea before making a mad dash to the next.

I do know one thing, however! It is time I find a way to get my life back on track, share myself with the Lord, listen to His direction and set myself on a right path forward.

I also know this experience has shown me the brain is really quite overpowering; it alerts me I have so much to share, and demands me to begin!

Today is January 7th, 2016. My brain is strong and alive at 3:00 AM and as I sit at my table, sharing my thoughts with you, I begrudge that part of my brain that will not allow me to rest. It seems to take control of me, giving me a wake-up call to document every aspect of this journey.

You know me... I am that same 64-year old woman who had a serious accident 12 ½ years ago. July 13th, 2003 seems such a long time ago at many levels, but there are times it is as though only a matter of days have passed me by. I still find myself experiencing that unsettled feeling within. I remember

Oh! The Journey | Bobbie R. Yeates

those questions so vividly! "Where has Bobbie gone? Is she ever going to return?"

As I sit here, sharing my pen with you, I am having a real "reality check!" The reality remains—brain trauma comes in many different forms—but it changes people forever! I am a different person today; some good—some bad. I really appreciate that you allow me to sort out some of these issues. For example: my feelings. I remember hearing people talk about wearing your feelings on your sleeves; heck, I often wear mine on top of almost everything! I cry too easy, knowing I am just not letting things go. And I ask you again, "Why? Is it normal for someone to take a simple issue of having their feelings hurt blow things all out of proportion and make the proverbial mountain out of a small molehill?

You know God has directed me to write a book and share this journey with a world of readers who need to rely on it for peace and direction. What I am feeling tonight is that He perhaps intends for me to put some closure on my experience and finally get on with my own life. If the book helps others—that is the bonus in life with which I would be blessed.

Can we have a little heart-to-heart here? I appreciate how you have constantly been so receptive to all I have to say—and never judged me! That unconditional concern over how I manage so many elements of traumatic brain injury has created the foundation for my next step... taking the leap! Writing the book, one step at a time. Well, we might have to look at moving forward one inch at a time, but you get the idea. I think I am finally ready to listen to God's voice.

My communication was often to the Diary of my journaling. I found comfort there, contentment in a world of confusion. Some days my posts were short snippets as I knew I didn't want to lose the thoughts; other days, I am sure had my diary been a living thing, would have noted how I wandered about, with my thoughts having no direction as I released what bothered me, and what surfaced in the process.

Dear Friend,

Here I am again, listening to my heart as it tells me...

> *Follow your heart wherever it takes you, and be happy.*
>
> *Life is brief and very fragile and only loaned us for a while.*
>
> *Wake up every morning with the thought that something wonderful is about to happen!*

It also speaks to me of my family, saying as Robert Woodward so wisely counseled...

> *There is nothing like family.*
>
> *Our memories sustain us through whatever life may bring.*
>
> *We are connected by this... that neither time nor distance can alter.*

I am not the least bit surprised it reminds me I committed to write everyday! I do plan on writing because I have yet so much to say, but I don't... do you suppose it is because it dredges up so many levels of emotion? What do you think, my friend?

Oh! The Journey | Bobbie R. Yeates

Dear Friend,

Well, here I am again! Thank you for being my comfort.

What a day! I woke up late—almost 8:30—and I had babysitting charges at 9:30. But I got ready for Brooklyn and played with her... taking her for a walk, watered plants, had breakfast and just had fun. Around 11:30 Maygen and Brooklyn left and I went to get a shirt and shoes for Garth. But, when I held it up, looking at him, I got so dizzy I almost fell over. I could not get my bearings, and I must tell you—I got really scared—and all I could think of was finding a place where I could lie down.

But you know me... I then opted to clean my kitchen, even though I felt really odd. My head felt like someone was pushing on it so I gave in to reason and went downstairs and slept until after two. When I woke up, imagine my dismay! My head was still not right. The "heavy head" did get better and I later cut Debbie's hair and talked about every thing, but particularly my fears about the pills and my seizures. So many questions about pills that seem to harm me, and why I need them. Or what do I need instead?

Oh! The Journey | Bobbie R. Yeates

May 3, 2016

Well, Friend, can you believe so many years have gone by? I just wanted to stop in and share with you that I had a truly wonderful day! I took another "step" Friday; it felt wonderful to go on a razor ride with Garth. I did not get nervous or feel filled with anxiety; I just relaxed and enjoyed it.

May 4th

Oh! No! I had some weird kind of attack in the night; left me wondering if I was sleep walking... the doors have been opened.

GOING SOCIAL

SOCIAL MEDIA STILL overwhelms me, but with the support of a dear friend who believes in me, and that the messages throughout *Oh! The Journey* should be shared with an awaiting audience, I opened my mind to the possibilities. The following include some of the messages I felt compelled to share as they became a part of my "journaling" activities. Actually, the creative part of me rather enjoys mixing the words with the images!

SOMETIMES, WHEN I feel I am in this brain fog of confused thinking about what I am experiencing, it helps to look at the "facts" about Traumatic Brain Injury. I am **not alone**; I am not totally different than everyone else!

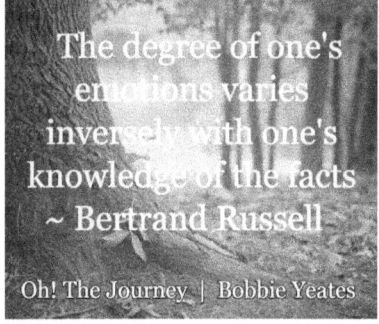

The degree of one's emotions varies inversely with one's knowledge of the facts
~ Bertrand Russell

Did you know... the Centers for Disease Control & Prevention's last report for TBI experienced in the United States reflected, an estimated 1.7 million people sustain a TBI annually. Of them:

52,000 die,
275,000 are hospitalized, and

1.365 million, nearly 80%, are treated and released from an emergency department.

TBI is a contributing factor to a third (30.5%) of all injury-related deaths in the United States.

About 75% of TBIs that occur each year are concussions or other forms of mild traumatic brain injury (MTBI)

Direct medical costs and indirect costs of TBI, such as lost productivity, totaled an estimated $60 billion in the United States.

Startling, aren't they? One of my dear friends shared she had a conversation with someone—wondering if there was a large enough "audience" for *Oh! The Journey*... and if you look at the numbers of events, and multiply that by peers, friends, family members and loved ones who are also impacted... I would say the answer is an unequivocal, "Yes!"

So, I encourage you to pick up a good book—well, actually lots of them! There are more messages of clarity and encouragement than you can imagine... just waiting there for you, like this one, to move you one step closer to a life well-lived.

WHAT DO YOU do when you have a bad day and just need a "shot of hope?" I try to look outside my current circumstances, and myself and sometimes, although many people might not agree, after more than a decade of experiencing the TBI results, I feel qualified to share with others who suffer... traumatic brain injuries are the most devastating injury possible.

The bruises, the breaks and cuts—they are visible and far more easily treatable. It is the invisible damage that makes life difficult; physical *and* cognitive impairment that mess with memories and communication are even small when compared to what it is like to no longer feel like yourself.

Not to be morbid, but it has at times fascinated me that brain injuries affect people of every age, race, religion, social class, and even political party. Here I was, a relatively unknown person in a small western town—suddenly thrown in with sports stars, comedians, athletes, award-winning musicians, and politicians. They struggle equally with the same challenges every traumatic brain injury victim faces.

I thought I might see just who was rich and famous who suffered TBI and found a fascinating site that lists several. This one most captivated me and yes, gave me hope!

"Okay, he may not be a modern celebrity, but President Lincoln was one of the most famous people to ever lead the United States, and he suffered a serious head injury long before he became a national leader. He was just 10 years old when a mule or horse kicked  him in the forehead and knocked him unconscious. He was out for hours. Young Lincoln didn't have the benefit of today's medical technology, but evidence suggests that he may have fractured his skull. What's certain is that Lincoln did suffer symptoms characteristic of a traumatic brain injury throughout his life, from impaired vision to depression and even weakness in the facial muscles on his left side. The good—inspiring, even—news is that Lincoln's brain injury didn't prevent him from becoming president. While a TBI is often life-changing, it doesn't have to mean giving up hope."

Citation: http://www.myinjuryattorney.com/.../7-celebrities-who-suffer.../

I CAN WELL empathize with those who feel they live life on the edge...

So much of the journey through traumatic brain injury is emotional. We are forever changed by an invisible force, which conjures up all nature of emotions that throw our lives off kilter. Once in a while, a reality check is called for—we need to know—not just suppose or take hearsay as valid—what we are actually being called upon to deal with!

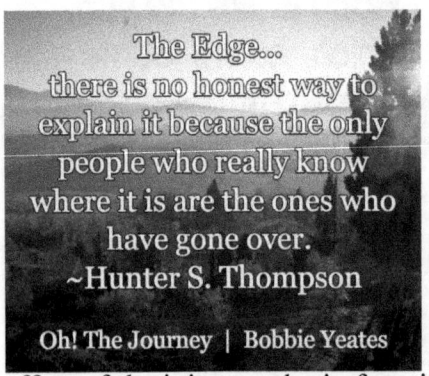

The Edge... there is no honest way to explain it because the only people who really know where it is are the ones who have gone over.
~Hunter S. Thompson

Oh! The Journey | Bobbie Yeates

So many cases of TBI are either not diagnosed, or, in the lack of adequate communication, not fully understood. According to an article, which I recently read on the Mayo Clinic site, "The terms "mild," "moderate" and "severe" are used to describe the effect of the injury on brain function. A mild injury to the brain is, however, is still a serious injury that requires prompt attention and an accurate diagnosis."

Let me repeat what caught me...

A mild injury to the brain is still a serious injury that requires prompt attention and an accurate diagnosis!

Oh! The Journey | Bobbie R. Yeates

You have no idea how many years my emotions have seen probably far more damaged than necessary because there was a mis-understanding that mild trauma was not all that bad a thing to deal with! During a recent medical visit, I learned (once again) that I am fortunate to even be alive today... the damage having been quite severe—and yet my understanding was my injury was diagnosed as mild. My heart is far less burdened today, knowing my physical and mental pain were far from imagined, and the behavioral changes far removed from my ability to fix them!

Don't live on the edge; don't suffer needlessly—have a real heart to heart with the professionals who can "tell it like it is" so you can manage life more easily in the face of that honest knowledge.

FINDING CLARITY IN DOODLES

ANOTHER FUN AND engaging way to use your writing to find the answers to the many issues you face with traumatic brain injury is better known as doodling! The adult coloring books that are increasing in popularity are considered a valuable relaxation technique. Those of us who suffer with TBI are often are unable to let go of negative thoughts that invade our mind. Not being secure in ourselves, we constantly think about ways to fix situations but are unable to come up with anything, the result is simply more stress and worry.

I invite you to sit down and color! When you let the designs claim your focus, you will discover a mind—calm and clear—that opens you to receive answers and insights that were probably there all along, but had just been lost in your mind's chaos. If you search online, you may see it categorized under art therapy.

There is just something stress-busting when you sit down with simple images or messages filled with swirling lines, patterns, and shapes... just begging for you to color them in! In the middle of an anxiety attack; grab a doodle and let go of the perfectionist in you; nothing has to be realistic, nor colored in the way the rest of the world considers natural. The therapy will not only relax you, it might even expand your creativity. I have chosen a few doodles designed to inspire and motivate you—not only to give you a break, but also to encourage you to design your own "doodles" once you get the general idea.

You see, your thoughts, or words you use to anchor yourself or find focus, can become doodles as you write them out and fill in the space around them as you look for your calming place. Gone are the kindergarten days when you had to add a particular color to a specific block; here you will discover a new freedom as your possibilities expand.

You can doodle anywhere! Riding in the car, in the doctor's office as you wait, and wait, and wait; in bed at night when your insomnia kicks in and you want to settle your mind so you have a good night's sleep. No more do you need to feel all tensed up at the sight of a blank white page... it can be your anxiety reliever, where you can leave all fear behind you and live with the beautiful, bold and colorful page(s) you create as a Zen doodler!

The examples included here are courtesy: Doodle Art Gallery (http://www.mediafire.com/).

Oh! The Journey | Bobbie R. Yeates

Oh! The Journey | Bobbie R. Yeates

Oh! The Journey | Bobbie R. Yeates

WHAT WE REALLY do not need during an anxiety attack or sleepless nights are rules and complicated step-by-step directions that further stress us! In fact, there is a really famous TED Talk by Sunni Brown, who says "doodling is deep thinking in disguise; it is a simple, accessible tool for problem-solving in general." At the end of the day, we can use it as an escape, a distraction, and purposeful action, and we can return to the images we create... again and again, just because they came from our heart and we like them!

Since we often suffer from diminished memory, I found it interesting research suggests doodling is also helpful in memory retention. In one experiment (Andrade 2010) people were asked to listen to a phone message about an upcoming party and then write down the names of the people who would attend, and ignore those who would not. Half the people were to use circles and squares as they wrote the names; the other half was just to make a standard list. The results of the memory test later given to the entire group showed the doodlers who were allowed to use the circles and squares remembered 30% more names than the group who simply wrote out a list. The reason: doodling helps us to be more "in the moment!"

Oh! The Journey | Bobbie R. Yeates

ABOUT THE AUTHOR

Bobbie Yeates is an author, motivational speaker, and advocate of traumatic brain injury. Looking life full in the face following a severe accident in 2003, she shares her journey of hope and inspiration with others who experience a similar life-altering condition.

Retired from a lengthy career in the beauty industry, Bobbie resides with her husband in Riverton, Wyoming, and enjoys time with family, friends and children, and grandchildren.

Bobbie enjoys reading, sports, and traveling with her husband, Garth; she loves being a mother and grandmother, and just being free to "be"—wondering what the day will be bring, being with her husband or her family."

Discover more of Bobbie at www.mylifeisbydesign.com

Or email her at byeates@wyoming.com

Oh! The Journey | Bobbie R. Yeates

I am providing this space for you to place notes, as you read. Things you want to remember, things you may want to visit with me about, or things you may want to share with your family and/or friends. This space is a place for you to begin journaling...

_____

_____

_____

_____

_____

_____

_____

_____

_____

_____

_____

Oh! The Journey | Bobbie R. Yeates

Oh! The Journey | Bobbie R. Yeates

Oh! The Journey | Bobbie R. Yeates

Oh! The Journey | Bobbie R. Yeates

Oh! The Journey | Bobbie R. Yeates

www.ingramcontent.com/pod-product-compliance
Lightning Source LLC
Chambersburg PA
CBHW071720090426
42738CB00009B/1831